FAT

MW01006960

and
ULTRA LOW FAT
Recipes
from
DORIS'
KITCHEN

Doris Cross

First Printing August, 1991
Cover design by Joulia Cross
Printed by: Morris Press

ISBN 0-9631490-0-8

TO MY MOM

With Love

TABLE OF CONTENTS

ACKNOWLEDGMENTS

A very special thanks to Maurice Gershon, my good friend, who always supports my latest venture with love and enthusiasm.

Also, this cookbook would not have been possible without my lawyer and friend, Michael Morgan. His legal advise and personal support was invaluable. Thank you to his wife Valerie for testing recipes and her personal critique.

Thanks to Stella Gilbert and her computer expertise. She saved me many hours of tedious work! Stella & Kim Pryor came through for me when I needed them the most.

Kim Pryor played a very important role with her volunteer typing and enthusiasm and encouragement. She is the best taste tester ever.

Thank you to Hugh Merrill (Resource Enhancements, Inc.) and his wife Kathy for their help with my computer programs and Ann Johnston and Malinda McCormick for their contribution to the final stages of the cookbook.

A special thanks to Sue Sturgeon for her help and moral support.

Thank you to Maxine Kamm for her interest and encouragement.

And last, but not least, thanks to my son who says "I survived the tasting for one cookbook and I probably will survive this one too". I am grateful for all the dishes he and his wife, Joulia, washed and the help they gave me in the kitchen. Also, a very special thanks to Joulia Cross for the artwork & cover design.

FROM SOMEONE WHO HAS BEEN THERE

I LOST 100 POUNDS

Low fat does not mean tasteless and dry. It's wonderful! It is surprising what a person can do with a very small amount of lite sour cream, fat free cheese, or lite cream cheese to make an ordinary dish taste rich and sinful.

Five years ago I lost ONE HUNDRED POUNDS on a popular franchised diet plan. Losing the weight is only half the battle: keeping it off has been the real struggle. The most important thing I discovered along the way: It doesn't matter how well a diet works; if it is not compatible with your lifestyle, you will gain the weight back.

What I have attempted to do with this cookbook, is to make people aware that they can eat the foods they have grown to love over the years, and eat them ultra low fat.

I have found that low fat eating and cooking fits very comfortably with my lifestyle. Not to mention what it does for my heart, my arteries, and overall health.

The fat free mayonnaise and the fat free cheeses are the products that have contributed the most to making my life more enjoyable. These two particular products are main features in my cookbook.

In November, 1990, I decided to take my idea on the road. I opened my own Weight Loss Center and designed my own low fat diet plan. When my dieters started wanting recipes, I began working on the foods they craved, and I made them into low fat recipes so that they could enjoy eating and still lose weight.

Hence, the beginning of this cookbook. I have had a wonderful time working on the recipes and have eaten the most wonderful food in the process.

If you can eat delicious food and lose weight, why would anyone want to eat any other way? Besides making you fat, it clogs your arteries. I am sure that this cookbook is only the beginning of my adventures in ultra low fat cooking. So here's wishing you many years of healthy low fat cooking and I hope that you derive a great deal of pleasure from these recipes.

Sincerely,

Doris Cross

Doris Cross

P.S. I've found this absolutely wonderful new product. It's called "Buttermist". It has the same number of calories and same grams of fat as other non-stick cooking sprays, **except**--it tastes just like spraying butter out of a can. Use it like any other non-stick spray. On bread it makes heavenly garlic toast. Wonderful on popcorn. To order "Buttermist":

Doris' Diet Recipes, Inc.
P.O. Box 549
Stillwater, OK 74076
(405) 372-4105

Visa or Mastercard available on phone orders.
2 - 14 oz. cans, $11.00 plus $2.50 postage and handling.
Minimum order 2 cans.

SHOPPING AND COOKING GUIDE

For Ultra Low Fat and Fat Free Recipes

LEARN TO READ LABELS. This is one of the most important keys to cooking and eating the ultra low fat way.

Always check the grams of fat on any product label. Also note the serving size in relation to the number of grams of fat. If the label says 1 gram of fat per serving and the serving size is 1/24th of a small cake, then obviously the 1 gram is not a real bargain,
If the grams of fat are not listed on a particular product. Put it back on the shelf.

Read the list of ingredients on products that do have some fat added. The ingredients are listed in the order of how much is used in the product. So, the further down on the list the oil or fat is, the less there is in the product.

Always compare same types of lite products, made by different companies. There can be a huge difference in the amounts of fat. Or the label may say the same grams of fat, so they will compare the same, but the serving size on one will be half as much as the other. Every company wants their product to compare favorable, in grams of fat with their counterparts. So, they fool you by changing the serving size.

The grams of fat in flour tortillas can range from 2 grams of fat per serving to 5 or 6 grams per serving. Some are low, some are not.

Some skim milk has 1 gram of fat per serving. Some has 0 grams per serving.

Some white flour has 1 or 2 grams of fat per serving. Some has 0 grams of fat.

Not all liquid egg substitutes are alike, even though they may all say no cholesterol. This does not always mean no fat. Most liquid egg substitutes are egg whites with a little coloring. However, some have used corn oil or some other type of oil to replace the fat lost in removing the yolk. Be sure and read the grams of fat and ingredients to check if oil has been added.

Beware of honey mustards, unless it is determined by reading the label that no oil has been added. Several honey mustards list the first ingredient as soybean oil.

When buying fat free cheese, be sure it is FAT FREE and not lite. There is a tremendous difference in grams of fat. Most lite cheeses are not a good choice. They are too high in fat.

Always read the label on fat free mayonnaise and make sure it says 0 grams of fat. There are so many LOW fat and REDUCED calorie dressings on the shelf that it is very easy to pick up the wrong one.

Canned chicken broth is virtually fat free, if you remove the small teaspoon of fat that floats on the top of the can, when it is opened.

Do not use regular canned soups for cooking or eating. Most are very high in fat. There are only a few specialty item soups that are low fat. They will usually not be with the regular soup section of your store. Look in the section that stocks diet or specialty items.

Some baked items, made from scratch, that are baked in your oven, may not brown on top satisfactorily. This is due to the lack of fat in the recipe. If this happens, just place it under the broiler for a few minutes to brown the top. Watch carefully. It will burn quickly.

Do not use graham crackers that have already been ground. Find the brand with the lowest grams of fat and grind your own. The ones that have been ground for you are too high in fat. Also, there is a tremendous difference from one brand to another in grams of fat in graham crackers. Some have 1 gram and some have 3 grams per same serving size.

Notice the turkey bacon label. The grams of fat listed per serving is AFTER the bacon has been cooked. Always cook turkey bacon first, before adding it to a recipe, to get the lowest grams of fat per serving.

Fat free cheeses do not stand up well to extremely high temperatures. They scorch and burn easily because of the lack of fat in the cheese.

Note: Fat free cheeses freeze beautifully.

Special Note

A new, very low fat cheddar cheese is available from Vermont. I have tasted it and use it all the time. Only 2 grams of fat per ounce and it tastes and melts like real cheddar cheese. You really must taste it to believe it. Available by mail order: **Cabot Farms, 1-800-639-3198.**

Fat Free and
Ultra Low Fat

APPETIZERS,
DIPS & BREADS

Ultra Low Fat

RANCH DIP FOR VEGETABLES

1 large (24 oz.) carton 1% cottage cheese
8 T. lite sour cream
I 1 oz. package dry ranch dressing mix.
Raw vegetables: celery sticks, carrot sticks, green pepper etc. for dipping.

Use food processor and cream entire carton of cottage cheese until it becomes very smooth and creamy. Blend and cream for about 5 minutes or longer. Add lite sour cream. Blend until well mixed. Add dry ranch dressing mix and blend.

Serve as a dip for raw vegetables or use on baked potato. Also good with pretzels.

Entire recipe makes 8 servings.

Grams Of Fat Per Serving   Calories Per Serving
2   88

Ultra Low Fat

QUESADILLAS

2 small soft flour tortillas
1/2 cup *Alpine Lace Free & Lean* fat free cheese, shredded
1/4 cup chopped green chilies
1/4 cup chopped green onion
suggested garnishes: lite sour cream, chopped tomatoes, salsa

Preheat oven: 375°

Sprinkle 1 oz. cheese onto half of each flour tortilla. Add evenly on each, green onion and green chilies. Fold the empty half over the filled half to form a half moon. Place on baking sheet sprayed with non-stick cooking spray.   Bake at 375 degrees for 20-25 minutes. Remove and serve warm.

May be sliced in pie shaped sections and garnished with lite sour cream, chopped tomatoes, salsa, etc. Makes a great finger food for parties.

Entire recipe makes 2 servings.

Grams Of Fat Per Serving	Calories Per Serving
2	160

Ultra Low Fat

ONION-DILL DIP

1 cup 1% cottage cheese
2 T. lite sour cream
1/4 cup fat free mayonnaise
1 green onion, chopped
1/2 t. dill weed
1/4 t. garlic powder
Dash of tabasco sauce

In food processor whip cottage cheese to the consistency of sour cream. Add all remaining ingredients except chopped onion, and blend well. Remove from processor and add onion. Flavor is better if allowed to chill before serving.

Entire recipe makes 2 servings.

Grams Of Fat Per Serving	Calories Per Serving
2	140

CHILI CHEESE DIP

2 cups low fat chili (made from recipe in this book)
See Index
2 T. lite sour cream
1/2 cup water
1 cup *Alpine Lace Free & Lean* fat free cheese, shredded

Additional items that can be added after cheese is melted:

chopped fresh onion
chopped jalapenos
chopped green chilies

In small saucepan heat chili, lite sour cream, water and cheese. Stir over low heat till cheese is thoroughly melted. Remove from heat and serve or add any additional items from list above. Serve as a dip with fat free tortilla chips. Great for a party.

Entire recipe makes 6 servings.

<u>Grams Of Fat Per Serving</u>   <u>Calories Per Serving</u>
            1   156

CORNBREAD AND BLACKEYED PEA BAKE

1 15 oz. can blackeyed peas
1 lb. ground turkey breast or chicken breast, browned
1 cup yellow cornmeal
1 cup low fat buttermilk
1/2 t. soda
1 t. salt
2 t. baking powder
3 egg whites, slightly beaten
1 cup corn, drained
1/2 cup chopped onion
1 cup *Alpine Lace Free & Lean* fat free cheese, shredded
1/3 cup green chilies, chopped

Preheat oven: 350°

In large bowl, combine dry ingredients and mix. First add buttermilk and then all remaining ingredients and stir. Pour into large shallow baking dish, sprayed with non-stick cooking spray. Bake at 350 degrees for 40-45 minutes.

Entire recipe makes 8 servings.

Grams Of Fat Per Serving	Calories Per Serving
2	285

Ultra Low Fat

ONION CHEESE BREAD

2 3/4 cups flour
1/4 t. soda
1 pkg. rapid rise yeast
3/4 T. sugar
1 t. salt
1 cup low fat buttermilk
1/2 cup 1% cottage cheese
4 T. lite sour cream
1 T. dry onion flakes
1 egg white, slightly beaten
1 cup *Alpine Lace Free & Lean* fat free cheese, shredded

Preheat oven: 350°

Combine dry ingredients, including yeast, and mix. Heat buttermilk until hot. DO NOT BOIL. Combine cottage cheese and lite sour cream and mix. Add this mixture to warmed buttermilk and stir. Add buttermilk mixture and egg white to dry ingredients and stir. Add cheese and mix thoroughly. Place bowl in slightly warm place and let rise till dough is doubled in size. After rising, stir dough with large spoon and pour into loaf pan sprayed with non-stick cooking spray. Let dough rise again, until about double in size, or until well above the top of the loaf pan. Place in oven and bake at 350 degrees for 50 minutes. Remove and cool on a rack. Do not slice immediately.
Entire loaf makes 12 large servings.

Grams Of Fat Per Serving	Calories Per Serving
less than 1	143

Ultra Low Fat

CHEESE DROP BISCUITS

2 cups flour
1/2 t. salt
1/2 t. soda
1 T. baking powder
1 t. sugar
1 egg white, slightly beaten
1 cup low fat buttermilk
1 cup *Alpine Lace Free & Lean* fat free cheese, shredded

Preheat oven: 400°

Combine dry ingredients for dough and mix. Combine buttermilk with egg white and mix. Add buttermilk and egg mixture to flour and stir. Add cheese and mix well. Drop, by large spoonful, onto baking sheet sprayed with non-stick cooking spray and bake at 400 degrees for about 15 minutes. If the top of the biscuits do not brown, place under broiler for a few seconds to brown the tops. Serve.

Entire recipe makes 8-10 servings, depending on the size of each biscuit.

Grams Of Fat Per Serving
less than 1

Calories Per Serving
151

Fat Free

CHEESE PUFFS

3 egg whites
1 T. flour
1/2 t. salt
1 cup *Alpine Lace Free & Lean* fat free cheese, shredded
1 cup fat free cracker crumbs (Use fat free saltines)
1/4 t. garlic powder

Preheat Oven: 350°

Beat egg whites until stiff. In a separate bowl, combine cheese, flour, salt, and garlic. Fold cheese mixture into egg whites. Form into walnut sized balls and roll each ball in fat free cracker crumbs. Bake in 350 degree oven 20-25 minutes or until golden brown.

Entire recipe makes 6 servings.

Grams Of Fat Per Serving   Calories Per Serving
0   88

Ultra Low Fat

COCKTAIL SAUSAGE & CHEESE BALLS

1 lb. ground turkey sausage
1 cup *Alpine Lace Free & Lean* fat free cheese, shredded
2 cups flour
1/2 t. salt
1/4 cup low fat buttermilk
1/2 t. soda
1 T. baking powder
1 egg white, slightly beaten

Preheat oven: 350°

In medium sized bowl, combine flour, soda, baking powder, and salt and mix thoroughly. In large bowl, combine turkey sausage, shredded cheese, buttermilk and egg white. Add about 1/2 cup of flour, at a time, to meat mixture and stir. Alternate add 1/2 cup flour to meat mixture and combining until all flour has been mixed in. Mixing is easier if done with your hands instead of a spoon. When thoroughly mixed and all flour is added, roll into walnut sized balls and place on baking sheet sprayed with non-stick cooking spray. Bake at 350 degrees for 40 minutes. Serve warm. May be refrigerated or frozen and reheated in microwave.

Entire recipe makes 10 servings.

Grams Of Fat Per Serving   Calories Per Serving
6   208

Fat Free

TARTAR SAUCE

1/2 cup fat free mayonnaise
1 T. lemon juice
1/2 t. dry onion flakes
1 T. chopped sweet or dill pickle or relish (optional)

In small bowl, mix all ingredients. Serve with fish.

Entire recipe makes 2 servings.

<u>Grams Of Fat Per Serving</u>   <u>Calories Per Serving</u>
0   50

Fat Free

ARTICHOKE MARINADE

1 cup fat free Italian salad dressing
1 small onion
1 14 oz. can artichoke hearts, water packed
1/4 t. garlic powder

Puree onion in food processor. Add salad dressing and garlic and mix thoroughly. Drain water from artichoke hearts. Pour artichokes in bowl or jar and add marinade. Cover and refrigerate overnight or for several hours. Use in salads and rice dishes or as a garnish for other dishes.

Entire recipe makes 2-4 servings.

Grams Of Fat Per Serving
0

Calories Per Serving
101

MAURICE'S CHEESE TOAST

3 English muffins cut in half
1/2 cup *Alpine Lace Free & Lean* fat free cheese,
shredded
1 T. lite sour cream
1 T. fat free mayonnaise
1/8 t. minced garlic

In small bowl mix fat free cheese lite sour cream, fat free mayonnaise and garlic. Stir until well blended. Set aside.

Spray baking sheet with non-stick cooking spray. Place muffins bottom side up on baking sheet and toast under broiler until brown. Be careful not to burn them. Remove pan from broiler and turn muffins over and return to broiler to toast the other side. When both sides are toasted, remove from broiler and spread each muffin with cheese mixture. Return to broiler just long enough to melt the cheese. Remove and serve.

Entire recipe makes **3** servings.

Grams Of Fat Per Serving	Calories Per Serving
1	188

HOMEMADE OIL FREE TORTILLA CHIPS

4 soft corn tortillas
Butter flavor non-stick cooking spray
Salt

Preheat oven: 350°

Use kitchen scissors and cut tortillas (2 at a time, if you want) in half and then cut each half into triangles. Place on baking sheet sprayed with butter flavored non-stick cooking spray. Sprinkle salt over chips and then spray chips very lightly with non-stick cooking spray. Bake in 350 degree oven for 12-13 minutes. These burn easily, so watch carefully.

Entire recipe makes 4 servings.

Grams Of Fat Per Serving
less than 1

Calories Per Serving
50

SOUR CREAM & CHEESE PANCAKES

3/4 cup lite pancake mix
2/3 + 1 T. water
1/2 cup *Alpine Lace Free & Lean* fat free cheese, shredded
2 T. lite sour cream
pinch of salt

Combine pancake mix and water according to package directions. Stir in lite sour cream and shredded cheese. Prepare grill or skillet with non-stick cooking spray and warm over med-high heat. When grill is hot, pour about 1/4 to 1/3 cup of batter on grill for each pancake. Cook about 2 minutes on each side or until brown.

Entire recipe makes 8 small pancakes.

Grams Of Fat Per Serving	Calories Per Serving
less than 1	39

Ultra Low Fat

CHEESE, ONION & DILL BAGEL

3 bagels, sliced in half
1/2 cup *Alpine Lace Free & Lean* fat free cheese, shredded
2 T. fat free mayonnaise
1 t. lemon juice
1/8 t. dill weed
1/8 cup onion, chopped
1/4 t. garlic powder
2-4 drops tabasco sauce

Blend together the fat free mayonnaise, lemon juice, dill weed, onion, garlic powder, tabasco. Add fat free cheese and mix. Toast plain bagels under broiler until slightly brown. Remove and spread each bagel with cheese mixture. Place back under the broiler for a minute or two or just long enough for cheese to melt.

Entire recipe makes 6 servings.

Grams Of Fat Per Serving
less than 1

Calories Per Serving
103

21

Fat Free

ARTICHOKE DIP

1 14 oz. can artichoke hearts, water packed
1 4 oz. can chopped green chilies
1 cup *Alpine Lace Free & Lean* fat free cheese, shredded
1/4 t. garlic powder
1 cup fat free mayonnaise
1/2 t. lemon juice
Dash of tabasco sauce

Preheat oven: 350°

Place all ingredients except cheese in food processor and blend. Remove to bowl and stir in fat free cheese. Pour into 8" baking dish sprayed with non-stick cooking spray. Bake at 350 degrees for 25-30 minutes. Serve warm with fat free chips or fat free crackers

Entire recipe makes 5-6 servings.

Grams Of Fat Per Serving	Calories Per Serving
0	107

FRENCH TOAST

4 slices fat free bread
1/2 cup liquid egg substitute (must be 0 gms. of fat)
1/4 t. vanilla
1 t. sugar
Powdered sugar for garnish, if desired

In small bowl, combine egg, vanilla, and sugar. Stir until sugar is dissolved. Dip each side of the bread, lightly, in egg mixture. Do not soak. Place on baking sheet sprayed with non-stick cooking spray and place under broiler until brown. Turn slices over and brown the other side. Serve warm with a little powdered sugar if desired.

Entire recipe makes 4 servings.

Grams Of Fat Per Serving   Calories Per Serving
            0   56

BAKED CHEESE

3 cups dry curd cottage cheese
1 small onion, chopped fine
1/3 cup green pepper, chopped fine
3 egg whites, slightly beaten
1 t. salt
1 cup *Alpine Lace Free & Lean* fat free cheese, shredded
1/4 t. garlic powder
1/2 t. lemon juice

Preheat oven: 300°

Drain as much water was possible out of the cottage cheese. In large bowl, combine cottage cheese, egg whites, salt, garlic powder and lemon juice. Beat with electric mixer for 1 minute. Add chopped onion, green pepper and shredded cheese. Stir until mixed thoroughly. Spray a 9" pie plate with non-stick cooking spray and pour mixture into pie plate. Bake at 300 degrees for 45 minutes. Serve warm with crackers or serve as a side dish with a meal. Great for parties. May be refrigerated and warmed in the microwave later.

Entire recipe makes 8 servings.

Grams Of Fat Per Serving   Calories Per Serving
less than 1   106

Ultra Low Fat

QUESO CHEESE DIP

1 cup *Alpine Lace Free & Lean* fat free cheese, shredded
1 10 oz. can Weight Watchers cream of mushroom soup
2 T. onion, chopped fine
1/2 cup fresh tomatoes, chopped
1 T. green chilies, chopped
4 T. lite sour cream

Combine all ingredients in sauce pan and simmer over very low heat until cheese has melted. Serve hot. Dip with any low fat cracker or oil free tortilla chips or pretzels. Great for a party.

Entire recipe makes 8 servings.

Grams Of Fat Per Serving
less than 1

Calories Per Serving
60

RANCH SEASONED BAGEL CHIPS

2 bagels
2 egg whites, slightly beaten
1 1 oz. package dry ranch dressing mix
Butter flavor non-stick cooking spray

Preheat oven: 400°

Stand a bagel on it's edge and carefully slice 1/4"
slices horizontally. Each bagel should make 5-6
slices. Spray a large baking sheet with butter flavor
non-stick cooking spray. Using a pastry brush, paint
both sides of each bagel slice lightly with egg white,
do not soak. Place slices on baking sheet and
sprinkle with dry ranch dressing mix. Spray lightly
with non-stick cooking spray and bake at 400
degrees for 4-5 minutes. Turn each slice and bake
another 5-6 minutes or until golden brown. Allow to
cool and store in air tight container. Try different
kinds of seasonings using the same method.

Other Suggested Seasonings
Molly McButter Sour Cream
Molly McButter Bacon Flavor
Salt and Dill Weed
Salt and Garlic

Entire recipe makes 4 servings.

Grams Of Fat Per Serving	Calories Per Serving
1	86

Ultra Low Fat

BROCCOLI CHEESE DIP

1 10 oz. pkg. frozen chopped broccoli
1 cup *Alpine Lace Free & Lean* fat free cheese, shredded
1 10 oz. can Weight Watchers Cream of Mushroom Soup
4 T. lite sour cream
1 t. dry onion flakes
1/8 t. garlic powder
Dash seasoned salt
Dash tabasco

Cook broccoli according to package directions and drain. Heat soup in medium sized sauce pan. As soup is heating, add remaining ingredients. Stir over low heat until cheese is melted. Serve warm.

Entire recipe makes 6 servings.

Grams Of Fat Per Serving   Calories Per Serving
    less than 1   88

Ultra Low Fat

PARTY SPINACH ROLLS

6 T. lite cream cheese
4 T. lite sour cream
1 green onion, chopped
1/2 of 1 oz. pkg ranch dressing mix (dry)
1/3 cup fat free mayonnaise
2 cups chopped frozen spinach
Dash of seasoned salt
Black pepper to taste
6 small flour tortillas

Squeeze and drain moisture from spinach. In medium sized bowl combine all ingredients except tortillas. Mix until well blended. Spread mixture on each flour tortilla and roll up into a log. Place each roll with seam down in dish. Refrigerate all rolls for several hours. Slice in 1/4" slices and serve.

Entire recipe makes 8 servings.

Grams Of Fat Per Serving
2

Calories Per Serving
112

28

BAKED CHEESE WITH HORSERADISH AND BACON

3 cups dry curd cottage cheese
1 small onion, chopped fine
2 slices turkey bacon, cooked and chopped
1 1/2 t. horseradish
3 egg whites, slightly beaten
1 t. salt
1 cup *Alpine Lace Free & Lean* fat free cheese, shredded
1/4 t. garlic powder
1/2 t. lemon juice

Preheat oven: 300°

Drain as much water was possible out of the cottage cheese. In large bowl, combine cottage cheese, egg whites, salt, garlic powder, horseradish and lemon juice. Beat with electric mixer for 1 minute. Add chopped onion, cooked turkey bacon and shredded cheese and stir until mixed thoroughly. Spray a 9" pie plate with non-stick cooking spray and pour mixture into pie plate. Bake at 300 degrees for 45 minutes. Serve warm with crackers or serve as a side dish with a meal. Great for parties. May be refrigerated and warmed in the microwave later.

Entire recipe makes 8 servings.

Grams Of Fat Per Serving	Calories Per Serving
1	112

Ultra Low Fat

SAUSAGE BALLS IN BARBECUE SAUCE

1 lb. ground turkey breast or chicken breast
1 egg white, slightly beaten
1/2 t. sage
1/2 t. crushed red pepper
1/8 t. nutmeg
1/4 t. dry mustard
1/2 t. black pepper
1/4 t. garlic powder
1/2 t. liquid smoke
1/2 t. salt
1 t. caraway seeds
2 cups barbecue sauce
1 small onion, chopped fine
Pinch of marjoram

Combine all ingredients, except barbecue sauce, in large bowl and mix thoroughly. Roll mixture into walnut sized balls and brown in a skillet sprayed with non-stick cooking spray. After browning on all sides, add barbecue sauce and simmer for 4-5 minutes. Serve warm. May be used for a party and served with toothpicks for easy handling.

Entire recipe makes 6 servings.

Grams Of Fat Per Serving
1

Calories Per Serving
202

30

CHOPPED SPINACH DIP

1 cup frozen, chopped spinach, thawed and drained
1/3 cup fat free mayonnaise
1/3 cup lite sour cream
1/2 cup onion, chopped
2 t. lemon juice
1/4 t. dill weed
Few drops lite soy sauce
2 t. dry ranch dressing mix
Dash of seasoned salt
Dash of tabasco sauce

Make sure spinach is drained thoroughly. Combine all ingredients in medium size bowl and mix. Chill before serving.

Entire recipe makes 4 servings.

Grams Of Fat Per Serving	Calories Per Serving
1	60

Ultra Low Fat

SLOPPY JOE DIP

1 lb. ground turkey breast or chicken breast
6 T. lite sour cream
2 green onions, chopped
1/2 cup barbecue sauce
1 t. prepared mustard
1/2 t. salt
Dash of garlic
Black pepper to taste

Brown ground turkey or chicken and onion in skillet sprayed with non-stick cooking spray. Simmer until done (about 10 minutes). Add all remaining ingredients. Stir and simmer 10 minutes. Serve warm.

Entire recipe makes 6 servings.

Grams Of Fat Per Serving	Calories Per Serving
2	135

32

Ultra Low Fat

TUNA PARTY BALL

3 6 oz. cans water packed tuna
1 8 oz. package or carton lite cream cheese
1 T. onion, grated or chopped fine
1/4 t. liquid smoke
1/4 t. seasoned salt
2 t. lemon juice
1 1/2 t. horseradish
1/2 cup *Alpine Lace Free & Lean* fat free cheese,
shredded
1/2 cup chopped parsley

In large bowl, combine all ingredients, except parsley. Mix thoroughly. Form into large ball and roll in chopped parsley. Chill and serve.

Entire recipe makes 12 servings.

Grams Of Fat Per Serving   Calories Per Serving
             2   81

Ultra Low Fat

GARLIC AND DILL DIP

1 cup fat free mayonnaise
4 T. lite sour cream
1/4 t. garlic powder
1/4 t. dry onion flakes
1 t. lemon juice
1/4 t. dill weed
1/2 t. tabasco sauce

Combine all ingredients in a small bowl and mix. Serve with fat free crackers or your own low fat bagel chips.

Entire recipe makes 4 servings.

Grams Of Fat Per Serving
1

Calories Per Serving
69

Ultra Low Fat

CREAMY HORSERADISH SAUCE

Use as a spread or heat and pour over meat or vegetables.

3/4 cup fat free mayonnaise
1 t. lemon juice
1/2 t. prepared horseradish
4 T. lite sour cream
Dash of garlic powder

Combine all ingredients in a small bowl and mix.

Entire recipe makes 4 servings.

Grams Of Fat Per Serving	Calories Per Serving
1	57

Ultra Low Fat

POTATO SKINS

1 potato
1 T. green onion, chopped
Seasoned salt
Black pepper
Butter flavor non-stick cooking spray
2 T. lite sour cream

Bake one potato in microwave for 4-6 minutes. Remove from oven after baking. Wrap in foil and let stand 5-10 minutes. Unwrap potato and cut in half length wise. Hot potatoes are easier to handle if allowed to cool at this point. Gently scrape out the insides of the potato out, do not scrape all the way to the skin....Leave a little potato around the edges and on the bottom. Reserve scrapings for another meal, if desired. Season potato skins with seasoned salt and pepper. Sprinkle green onion on each one. Place in small pan sprayed with butter flavor non-stick cooking spray. Lightly spray the potato skins with non-stick cooking spray so they will brown nicely. Place under broiler until golden brown.
Remove from broiler and spread inside of each potato skin with one tablespoon lite sour cream. Serve warm.

NOTE: If desired, mix 1-2 T. Ranch Dip (made from low fat recipe) with potato reserved from scraping. Mix well and season with some dry onion flakes, salt and pepper.

Entire recipe makes 2 serving.

Grams Of Fat Per Serving   Calories Per Serving
             2   128

JALAPENO CHEESE CORN BREAD

2 1/2 cups yellow cornmeal
2 1/2 cups low fat buttermilk
2 T. sugar
1/2 t. salt
3/4 t. baking soda
1 T. baking powder
2 egg whites, beaten (not stiff)
1/4 cup chopped jalapeno peppers (or green chilies, if you prefer   a milder taste)
1 cup *Alpine Lace Free & Lean* fat free cheese, shredded

Preheat oven: 400°

In large bowl, mix all dry ingredients. Stir until mixed well and set aside. In a small bowl, combine egg whites and buttermilk.   Add this mixture to dry ingredients and mix. Add peppers and stir. Reserve cheese for layer in center of batter. Spray 9" square pan with non-stick cooking spray. Pour in half the batter.   Sprinkle the cheese evenly over entire surface of batter. Pour remaining batter on top of cheese layer. Bake at 400 degrees for 30 to 35 minutes. The cornbread will probably not be brown on top at this point even though it is done. Remove from oven and spray top lightly with non-stick cooking spray. Place under broiler a minute or two to brown the top. Remove and serve. Note: Most baked breads will not brown very well without some extra help because of the lack of fat in the recipe.

Entire recipe makes 12 servings.

Grams Of Fat Per Serving	Calories Per Serving
1	156

BAGELS WITH CHEESE
& PIZZA SAUCE

2 bagels, sliced
4 T. pizza sauce
4 slices *Alpine Lace Free & Lean* fat free cheese
Garlic powder to taste

<u>Extra Optional Toppings</u>
Sliced mushrooms
Chopped onion
Chopped green pepper

Place bagels on baking sheet sprayed with non-stick cooking spray and place under broiler and toast lightly on each side. Remove from broiler and spread each bagel half with 1 T. pizza sauce. Cover with 1 slice of cheese and any optional ingredients. Place under broiler until cheese is melted. Great for a quick lunch or dinner.

Entire recipe makes 4 servings.

<u>Grams Of Fat Per Serving</u>	<u>Calories Per Serving</u>
less than 1	119

Ultra Low Fat

CRAB RANGOON

12 won ton wrappers
12 t. lite cream cheese
2 egg whites, slightly beaten
6 oz. cooked crab meat (can also use imitation crab or lobster)

Options To Add To Above Filling:

Green pepper, chopped very fine
Onion, chopped very fine

Preheat Oven: 375°

Dip only one side of the won ton wrappers in egg white. The egg dipped side will be on the outside and the dry side will be for the filling. Place on plate or saucer while adding the filling. Use 1 teaspoon lite cream cheese and a bite sized piece of crab meat for each filling. Add green pepper or onion if desired. Grasp the corners of the won ton wrapper bringing them all together at the top. Gently press the top closed. The ends should come to a point and stick straight up. Repeat for all remaining wrappers. Place on baking sheet sprayed with non-stick cooking spray. Bake in 375 degree oven for 9-10 minutes or until browned. Serve immediately.

Entire recipe makes 4 servings.

Grams Of Fat Per Serving   Calories Per Serving
           2   106

Ultra Low Fat

CHEESE LOG

1 8 oz. package or carton lite cream cheese
1 cup *Alpine Lace Free & Lean* fat free cheese, shredded
1/4 cup onion, chopped
1/4 cup green pepper, chopped
1/8 t. seasoned salt
1/8 t. garlic powder
1/4 cup fat free mayonnaise
3/4 cup fat free pretzels, crushed

Combine all ingredients except pretzels in large bowl. Mix thoroughly. Mold into log and roll log in crushed pretzels. Chill several hours before serving.

Entire recipe makes 8 servings.

Grams Of Fat Per Serving	Calories Per Serving
2	104

DILL & ONION SAUCE FOR BREAD
(Serve warm on bread or toast in place of butter)

1 small onion, sliced
1/2 cup Butter Buds (already mixed following pkg. directions)
1/4 t. + 1 sprinkle Molly McButter
1/4 t. dill weed
Dash of garlic
Dash of salt
Dash seasoned salt

Brown onion in small skillet sprayed with non-stick cooking spray. After onion is browned, reduce heat to very low and add remaining ingredients. Simmer over very low heat for 2-3 minutes. Spoon on hot bread or toast instead of butter.

Entire recipe makes 6 servings.

Grams Of Fat Per Serving
0

Calories Per Serving
14

41

Ultra Low Fat

SAUSAGE & CHEESE ROLL
(Makes little pinwheels, when cut and baked)

Filling
1 lb. ground turkey sausage
1 cup fat free-cheese, shredded
Seasoned salt

Dough
2 cups flour
1/2 t. salt
1/2 t. soda
1 T. baking powder
1 t. sugar
1 egg white, slightly beaten
1 cup low fat buttermilk

Preheat Oven: 400°

Combine dry ingredients for dough and mix thoroughly. Combine egg white with buttermilk and mix. Add buttermilk mixture to flour mixture and stir. Turn dough out onto floured surface and roll to 1/4 " thick. Use plenty of flour to keep rolling pin from sticking. Place small pieces of ground turkey over the entire top of rolled out dough. Sprinkle entire surface with shredded cheese.

Sprinkle entire surface very lightly with seasoned salt. Starting at one side, gently start to roll the dough into a long roll. Roll carefully and trying not to tear the dough. When finished rolling, lay roll on foil or plastic wrap. Wrap and place in refrigerator for at least 1 hour. Several hours is preferable. After chilling, slice log in 1/2 " pieces and place pieces on baking sheet sprayed with non-stick cooking spray. Bake at 400 degrees for 15 minutes or until golden brown. Remove and serve.

Entire recipe makes 12 serving.

Grams Of Fat Per Serving
5

Calories Per Serving
180

Ultra Low Fat

BACON AND CHEESE SPREAD

1 cup *Alpine Lace Free & Lean* fat free cheese, shredded
1/4 cup onion, chopped
4 T. lite cream cheese
1 T. fat free mayonnaise
1/4 t. horseradish
2 slices turkey bacon, cooked and crumbled

Combine all ingredients in small bowl and mix. Flavors are better if spread is refrigerated for several hours before serving. Serve on fat free crackers or use as a spread for sandwiches.

Entire recipe makes 8 servings.

Grams Of Fat Per Serving   Calories Per Serving
            1   54

Ultra Low Fat

CREAM CHEESE AND MUSHROOM SPREAD

1 8 oz. package or carton lite cream cheese
1/2 cup Weight Watchers Cream of Mushroom Soup
1/2 t. horseradish
1/4 t. garlic powder
1/2 cup canned mushrooms, drained and chopped
Dash of Worcestershire
Dash of seasoned salt
Dash of tabasco

Combine all ingredients in large bowl and mix thoroughly. Chill and serve. Wonderful on fat free crackers or no oil bagel chips.

Entire recipe makes 8 servings.

Grams Of Fat Per Serving | Calories Per Serving
2 | 48

Ultra Low Fat

SNACK MIX

1 1 oz. package dry ranch dressing mix
2 bagels, sliced
2 cups rice chex cereal
2 cups corn chex cereal
2 cups wheat chex cereal
2 cups fat free pretzels
2 t. sesame seeds
1/4 cup hot water
1 1/2 t. Molly McButter
1/4 t. seasoned salt

Preheat oven: 300 degrees

Slice bagels into small rounds. In large bowl, combine bagel rounds, all cereals and pretzels. Mix hot water with Molly McButter and pour into small spray bottle, if available. It is possible to sprinkle the water and butter mixture, but spraying is better. Alternately spray and then sprinkle ranch dressing mix on cereal mixture in large bowl. Spray a little on top, sprinkle on ranch dressing mix and a few sesame seeds. Toss cereal mixture. Repeat spraying and adding dressing mix and sesame seeds until all required amounts are used. To bake, use an extra large shallow baking dish or a baking sheet or roaster pan. Spray this container with non-stick cooking spray. Pour cereal mixture into large pan and bake at 300 degrees for 30-45 minutes. Stir midway through cooking time. Check frequently after 25 minutes, as this burns easily. Remove, cool and serve. Store in air tight container. Great for a party.

Entire recipe makes 10 servings.

Grams Of Fat Per Serving   Calories Per Serving
less than 1   142

Ultra Low Fat

RANCH CREAM CHEESE SPREAD

1 8 oz. package or carton lite cream cheese.
1 t. dry ranch dressing mix
1 t. dry onion flakes
1/2 t. lemon juice
2 T. green pepper, chopped
1/2 cup *Alpine Lace Free & Lean* fat free cheese, shredded

Combine in food processor lite cream cheese, ranch dressing mix, onion flakes and lemon juice. Process until mixed thoroughly. Remove from processor and stir in green pepper and fat free cheese. Serve chilled on fat free crackers.

Entire recipe makes 8 servings.

Grams Of Fat Per Serving   Calories Per Serving
            2   54

MEXICAN CORN FRITTERS

2 cups canned corn, drained
3/4 cup plus 2 T. flour
1/3 cup chopped green chiles
2 egg whites, slightly beaten
2 t. baking powder
1/2 cup skim milk
1 1/2 t. sugar
1/2 t. salt

Combine dry ingredients and stir thoroughly. Add all remaining ingredients and mix. Spray skillet with butter flavor non-stick cooking spray and warm over medium heat. Drop medium size spoonfuls of batter into skillet. Brown on one side, turn and brown on the other side. Repeat for remaining batter.

Entire recipe makes 6 servings.

Grams Of Fat Per Serving
0

Calories Per Serving
97

Fat Free

ITALIAN CHEESE, TOMATO AND GARLIC TOAST

4 thick slices fat free Italian bread
3/4 cup fat free mozzarella cheese
1 fresh tomato, sliced thin
1/2-1 t. sweet basil
1 clove fresh garlic, crushed
4 t. fat free Italian dressing
1 t. lemon juice

Place slices of bread on baking sheet sprayed with non-stick cooking spray and place under broiler until <u>lightly</u> brown on each side. Watch carefully - DO NOT BROWN VERY MUCH. In small bowl, combine cheese, lemon juice and garlic and toss until mixed. Sprinkle this mixture on each slice of bread. Place 1-2 thin slices of tomato on top of cheese. Sprinkle each piece with a little fat free Italian dressing and top with a few sprinkles of basil. Place back under broiler for 1-2 minutes or until cheese starts to melt. Remove and serve. Wonderful with salads for pasta meal.

Entire recipe makes 4 servings.

<u>Grams Of Fat Per Serving</u>
0

<u>Calories Per Serving</u>
100

HAM AND CREAM CHEESE ROLLS

6 slices low fat ham
4 T. lite cream cheese
2 T. chopped onion
2 T. chopped green pepper
1/2 t. lemon juice
1/4 t. garlic powder
Dash of tabasco
Dash of seasoned salt

Place ham slices on paper towels and blot to remove excess moisture. Combine all remaining ingredients in small bowl. Spread mixture on each ham slice. Roll ham slice into a log shape and slice for serving.

Entire recipe makes 6 servings.

Grams Of Fat Per Serving   Calories Per Serving
2   89

RANCH BREAD

7 cups bread flour
1 package dry yeast
1 1/2 t. salt
4 T. honey
3 cups buttermilk
2 1 oz. package dry ranch dressing mix
2 t. Molly McButter
1 T. dry onion flakes
1 T. fat free mayonnaise

Preheat oven: 350°

In sauce pan, combine honey, buttermilk, salt, Molly McButter, ranch dressing mix and fat free mayonnaise. Stir and warm mixture slightly - DO NOT BOIL. Set aside.

In large bowl combine 3 1/2 cups of flour with yeast and mix. Gradually add warm buttermilk mixture to flour and mix thoroughly. Gradually add almost all remaining flour (reserve 1/2 cup) and continue to mix. Turn dough out on floured surface and use remaining 1/2 cup flour while kneading dough when it becomes too sticky. Knead dough for 2-3 minutes.

Place dough in large bowl sprayed with non-stick cooking spray. Spray top of the dough lightly also -

cover with damp cloth and let rise until doubled (about 2 hours).

Punch dough down and divide into two pieces and shape into loaves and place in loaf pans sprayed with non-stick cooking spray. Let rise again until doubled (about 45 minutes). Bake at 350° for 50-60 minutes.

Entire recipe makes 2 loaves of bread.

Each loaf makes 12 servings.

Grams Of Fat Per Serving	Calories Per Serving
less than 1	116

Ultra Low Fat

MUSHROOM SOUP BREAD
WITH CHEESE

7 cups bread flour
1 package dry yeast
1 3/4 t. salt
3 T. honey
2 10 1/2 oz. cans Weight Watchers Cream of Mushroom Soup
1/4 cup water
1 cup *Alpine Lace Free & Lean* fat free cheese, shredded
2 T. dry onion flakes
2 t. Molly McButter

Preheat oven: 350°

In sauce pan, combine honey, mushroom soup, water, salt and dry onion flakes. Warm mixture slightly. In large bowl combine 3 1/2 cups of flour with yeast and mix. Gradually add soup mixture to flour and stir. Add cheese and mix thoroughly for several minutes. Gradually add almost all of remaining flour (reserve about 1/2 cup). Turn dough out on floured surface and knead and add remaining flour. Knead dough for 2-3 minutes.

Place dough in large bowl sprayed with butter flavor non-stick cooking spray. Cover and let rise until doubled (about 2 hours).

Punch dough down and divide in half. Shape into loaves and place in loaf pans that have been sprayed with non-stick cooking spray. Cover and let rise again until doubled (about **45** minutes to **1** hour).

Bake in **350°** oven for **50-60** minutes.

Entire recipe makes **2** loaves. Each loaf makes **12** servings.

<u>Grams Of Fat Per Serving</u>
less than 1

<u>Calories Per Serving</u>
142

Fat Free and Ultra Low Fat

SOUPS, SALADS, VEGETABLES

Ultra Low Fat

CREAMY GELATIN DESSERT OR SALAD

1 large (24 oz.) carton 1% cottage cheese
8 T. lite sour cream
1 small 0.3 oz. pkg. sugar free gelatin (any flavor)
6 pkgs. non-nutritive sweetener or 1/4 cup sugar
3 cups of fruit (any fruit)

Use food processor and cream entire carton of cottage cheese to the consistency of sour cream. A blender will work, but does not cream the cottage cheese as smooth as a food processor. Mix gelatin following package directions for dissolving. DO NOT ADD SECOND CUP OF WATER. Set dissolved gelatin aside to cool. Add sour cream to creamed cottage cheese and mix well. Add gelatin to cottage cheese and sour cream mixture. Add sweetener or sugar and mix. Fold in fruit. Pour in large glass casserole and place in refrigerator to chill. Takes at least 2 hours to set.

Entire recipe makes 8 servings.

Grams Of Fat Per Serving	Calories Per Serving
2	107

Suggested combinations:
Orange gelatin and mandarin oranges
Lime gelatin and pineapple
Strawberry gelatin and strawberries
Raspberry gelatin and raspberries
Raspberry gelatin and pineapple

Ultra Low Fat

HOT CHICKEN SALAD

12 oz. cooked boneless, skinless chicken breast, cut in chunks (about 4 small chicken breasts or use canned white chicken meat)
3 cups chopped celery
1 medium white onion, chopped
4 T. lite sour cream
1 cup *Alpine Lace Free & Lean* fat free cheese, shredded
1 cup fat free mayonnaise
2 T. lemon juice
1 1/2 cups crushed fat free pretzels for topping - measure after crushing
Couple of dashes of seasoned salt

Preheat oven: 375°

Mix lemon juice with fat free mayonnaise. Combine all ingredients except pretzels in large bowl. Stir until well mixed. Pour into 7" X 11" casserole dish sprayed with non-stick cooking spray. Sprinkle crushed pretzels on top and bake at 375 degrees for 25 minutes. Remove and serve.

Entire recipe makes 8 servings.

Grams Of Fat Per Serving	Calories Per Serving
1	164

Ultra Low Fat

WALDORF SALAD

2 1/2 cups apples, chopped
1 1/2 cups green seedless grapes
3/4 cup celery, chopped
1/2 cup fat free mayonnaise
6 T. lite sour cream
2 T. sugar
1/2 t. lemon juice
2 cups miniature marshmallows

In small bowl, combine fat free mayonnaise, lite sour cream, sugar and lemon juice. In large bowl combine apples, grapes and celery. Pour dressing over salad ingredients. Chill and serve. Stir in marshmallows just before serving.

Entire recipe makes 6 servings.

Grams Of Fat Per Serving   Calories Per Serving
1   106

SOUTHERN STYLE BAKED BEANS

3 15 oz. cans great northern or pinto beans (not pork
& beans)
3/4 cup onion, chopped
1/3 cup brown sugar
1/4 t. liquid smoke
1/2 cup catsup
1/3 cup water
3 slices turkey bacon

Preheat oven: 350°

Spray large skillet with non-stick cooking spray.
Brown the chopped onion. Cook turkey bacon in a
small skillet or in the microwave and set aside.
Combine all ingredients, except turkey bacon, in
large bowl and mix. Pour into large casserole dish,
sprayed with non-stick cooking spray. Place slices
of turkey bacon on top and bake at 350 degrees 35-
40 minutes.

Entire recipe makes 8 servings.

Grams Of Fat Per Serving   Calories Per Serving
            1   120

Ultra Low Fat

COLESLAW

3 cups cabbage, shredded or chopped
1 carrot, shredded or chopped
1/2 cup green pepper, chopped (optional)

OR

1 8 oz. can pineapple tidbits
1/2 cup raisins

Dressing:
1/2 cup fat free mayonnaise
6 T. lite sour cream
2 T. sugar
1/2 t. lemon juice
1 1/2 T. white vinegar

In small bowl, combine ingredients for dressing. In large bowl combine cabbage and carrot and other ingredients desired. Pour dressing over cabbage and mix.   Chill and serve.

Entire recipe makes 6 servings.

Grams Of Fat Per Serving   Calories Per Serving
1   68

Ultra Low Fat

BROCCOLI & CHEESE SOUP

1 cup canned evaporated skim milk
1 10 oz. can Weight Watchers cream of mushroom soup
2 cups frozen chopped broccoli
1/2 t. salt
1/2 t. dry onion flakes
1 cup skim milk
1 cup *Alpine Lace Free & Lean* fat free cheese, shredded
Black pepper to taste
Dash of garlic powder

In medium sauce pan, combine all ingredients and bring almost to a boil, stirring constantly. Reduce heat and simmer about 10 minutes or until cheese is melted. Stir frequently.

Entire recipe makes 6 servings.

Grams Of Fat Per Serving   Calories Per Serving
less than 1   123

CREAMED ASPARAGUS ON TOAST WITH CHEESE

2 cups cooked fresh asparagus
2 slices turkey bacon cooked
2 slices *Alpine Lace Free & Lean* fat free cheese
2 slices fat free bread, toasted

White Sauce:
2 T. flour
1 cup chicken broth (Use canned and remove fat from top)
1/2 t. dry onion flakes
2 T. lite sour cream
Salt and black pepper to taste

Spray a small sauce pan with non-stick cooking spray. Put flour in pan and gradually add enough broth to make a thin paste. Add sour cream and onions and salt and pepper if desired. Place over medium heat and stir constantly while gradually adding more broth. Continue stirring and cooking and adding broth until entire cup of broth is added. Continue cooking until mixture thickens. Set aside to pour over toast and asparagus.

Place toasted bread on plate and arrange asparagus on top of toast. Place cheese on top of asparagus and then place bacon on top of cheese. Pour about 1/2 cup of white sauce over top. Be sure the white sauce is hot enough to melt the cheese. Repeat for second piece of toast. Serve immediately.

Entire recipe makes 2 servings.

Grams Of Fat Per Serving	Calories Per Serving
2	149

Ultra Low Fat

CORN CHOWDER

3 slices turkey bacon, cooked and chopped
1 17 oz. can whole kernel corn
1 cup canned evaporated skim milk
4 T. lite sour cream
1 small onion chopped
1 cup chicken broth (use canned and remove fat from top)
1 cup water
1\4 t. Molly McButter
1\2 t. celery flakes
1\2 cup *Alpine Lace Free & Lean* fat free cheese, shredded
Salt and black pepper to taste

Spray medium sized saucepan with non-stick cooking spray. Brown onions until golden brown. Remove from heat and add sour cream. Stir while gradually adding broth and milk. Return to medium heat and add remaining ingredients. Simmer over very low heat for 5-10 minutes, stirring often. Remove and serve.

Entire recipe makes 4 servings.

Grams Of Fat Per Serving	Calories Per Serving
2	156

Ultra Low Fat

OLD FASHIONED POT OF BEANS

1 16 oz. small package dry beans, washed and drained
2 cloves fresh garlic or 1/4 t. garlic powder
1 cup chopped onion
4 slices turkey bacon, cooked
1/4 t. liquid smoke
1/4 t. black pepper
1 1/2 t. salt
2 cups water
5 cups fat free chicken broth (use canned and remove fat from top)
1/2 t. celery flakes
Dash of seasoned salt

NOTE: It is important to cook what little bit of fat is in the turkey bacon BEFORE adding it to the beans. This provides flavor without added fat.

Brown onion in skillet sprayed with non-stick cooking spray. Combine all ingredients in large pot. Simmer covered for 2-3 hours. Remove lid and cook another 30 minutes to 1 hour, until juice reaches desired consistency. Remove whole cloves of garlic before serving. Great with cornbread.

Entire recipe makes approximately 10 servings.

Grams Of Fat Per Serving   Calories Per Serving
2   180

CRISPY OVEN POTATO WEDGES

1 large potato, peeled
2 cups corn flakes, crushed
2 egg whites, slightly beaten
Seasoned salt

Preheat oven: 350°

Slice peeled potato in half length-wise. Take each half and slice into long strips or wedges, making about 4-5 pieces from each half. Dip each potato wedge in egg white and then roll in crushed corn flakes. Place wedges on a baking sheet sprayed with non-stick cooking spray. Sprinkle with seasoned salt and spray potatoes lightly with butter flavored non-stick cooking spray. Bake at 350 degrees for 35-40 minutes.

Entire recipe makes 2 servings.

Grams Of Fat Per Serving	Calories Per Serving
0	168

Ultra Low Fat

FROZEN CRANBERRY SALAD

1 16 oz. can jelled cranberry sauce
1 8 oz. can crushed pineapple
3 T. fat free mayonnaise
8 T. lite sour cream
2 cups 1% cottage cheese
2 T. sugar

In food processor, whip cottage cheese to the consistency of sour cream. Add fat free mayonnaise and lite sour cream. Process until mixed well. Add sugar and mix. Add cranberry sauce and process until smooth. Pour into large bowl and add pineapple. Stir until mixed thoroughly. Pour into 8" glass baking dish and freeze for several hours. Cut into 10 servings and serve.

Entire recipe makes 10 servings.

Grams Of Fat Per Serving   Calories Per Serving
          1   168

Fat Free

GAZPACHO

1 6 oz. can tomato paste
1 cucumber, peeled
2 cups chicken broth, (use canned and remove fat
from top)
2 cups water
1 small onion
1/4 t. salt
1/4 t. garlic powder
1/2 fresh green pepper
1 stalk celery, remove strings
Dash of tobasco sauce

In food processor, puree all ingredients, adding one
or two at a time until mixture is smooth. Remove
from processor to bowl and add water and mix well.
Chill and serve with cucumber slice in center.

Entire recipe makes 4 servings.

Grams Of Fat Per Serving   Calories Per Serving
             0   63

Ultra Low Fat

VICHYSSOISE

1 large potato, peeled and chopped fine
1 cup chicken broth (use canned and remove fat from top)
1 cup canned evaporated skim milk (0 gms. fat)
1 cup skim milk
4 T. lite sour cream
1 t. dry onion flakes
Chopped chives for garnish when ready to serve
Salt to taste

Combine all ingredients in medium sauce pan and simmer for 15 to 20 minutes or until potato is done. Cool for 15 minutes. Puree in food processor or blender until smooth. Chill and serve. Garnish with chopped chives.

Entire recipe makes 4 servings.

Grams Of Fat Per Serving   Calories Per Serving
              1   127

CREAMY FROZEN FRUIT SALAD

1 16 oz. can dark sweet cherries, pitted
1 8 oz. can crushed pineapple
1 8 oz. can pineapple tidbits
2 fresh bananas
1 cup lite cream cheese
1/4 cup fat free mayonnaise
1/3 cup sugar
1 1/2 cup 1 % cottage cheese
1 cup green seedless grapes

In food processor, combine lite cream cheese, cottage cheese, sugar, fat free mayonnaise and bananas until smooth.

Place grapes into large bowl. Drain all canned fruit and combine with grapes. Add creamed mixture to fruit and gently stir until mixed thoroughly.

Pour mixture into a large glass casserole baking dish and freeze for 4-6 hours. Thaw slightly before cutting into squares to serve.

Entire recipes makes 10 servings.

Grams Of Fat Per Serving	Calories Per Serving
2	156

CARROTS & ZUCCHINI
With Brown Sugar

1 1/2 cup carrots, shredded
1 1/2 cup zucchini, shredded
1 T. brown sugar
1/2 t. Molly McButter
1/4 cup water
Salt to taste

Spray large skillet with non-stick cooking spray. Add vegetables and sprinkle with brown sugar, Molly McButter, salt and saute. When skillet starts to get dry, add 1/4 cup water and continue to stir and simmer vegetables to desired tenderness.

Entire recipe makes **6** servings.

Grams Of Fat Per Serving	Calories Per Serving
0	30

LEMON HORSERADISH CREAM SALAD

1 small 3 oz. package lemon flavor gelatin
1/2 cup celery, chopped
8 T. lite cream cheese
3/4 t. prepared horseradish
1 T. onion, chopped
1/4 cup green pepper, chopped

Prepare lemon gelatin according to package directions. In a large bowl combine lite cream cheese and horseradish. Add a few tablespoons of prepared gelatin and continue to mix. Gradually add more gelatin until all gelatin is stirred into mixture. Add remaining ingredients and mix. Pour into individual molds or one large dish and chill for several hours until set.

Entire recipe makes 8 servings.

Grams Of Fat Per Serving   Calories Per Serving
            1   80

Ultra Low Fat

SAUERKRAUT SALAD

2 cups sauerkraut, drained
1/4 cup green pepper, chopped
1/2 small onion, chopped
2 stalks celery, chopped
1 T. chopped pimentos
1/4 cup carrot, grated
1 cup canned corn, drained
1 T. sugar

Combine all ingredients in large bowl and toss lightly. Cover and refrigerate several hours or overnight before serving.

Entire recipe makes 6 servings.

Grams Of Fat Per Serving   Calories Per Serving
       less than 1   71

TANGY CREAMED BROCCOLI

1 10 oz. package frozen broccoli
4 T. lite sour cream
1/3 cup fat free mayonnaise
1/2 t. dry onion flakes
1/4 cup skim milk
Salt to taste
Black pepper to taste

Cook broccoli as per package directions. In small saucepan, mix sour cream, mayonnaise, milk, onion flakes, salt and pepper together and simmer for 1 minute. Pour over cooked broccoli and serve.

Entire recipe makes 4 servings.

Grams Of Fat Per Serving   Calories Per Serving
            1   61

CHILLED CORN AND CHEESE SALAD

Salad:

2 15 oz. cans corn, drained
1 small onion, chopped
1/4 cup green pepper, chopped
1/2 cup *Alpine Lace Free & Lean* fat free cheese, shredded
1 T. chopped pimentos

Dressing:

1/2 cup fat free mayonnaise
1 t. lemon juice
1/8 t. garlic powder

-OR-

Alternate dressing:

1/2 cup fat free Italian dressing
1 t. lemon juice
1/8 t. garlic powder

In small bowl combine ingredients for dressing and mix. In large bowl, combine all ingredients for salad and mix. Pour dressing over salad and chill before serving.

Entire recipe makes 6 servings.

Grams Of Fat Per Serving   Calories Per Serving
       less than 1   71

CRAB PASTA SALAD

<u>Salad</u>:

2 cups cooked pasta
1 cup fresh broccoli, chopped fine
1 small carrot, grated
6 oz. cooked crab meat
1 T. onion, chopped fine
1/2 t. parsley flakes

<u>Dressing</u>:

1/2 cup fat free mayonnaise
2 t. lemon juice
Dash seasoned salt
3 T. water
Dash tabasco sauce
Dash of garlic powder

In small bowl combine all ingredients for dressing and mix. In large bowl combine all ingredients for salad and mix. Pour dressing over salad and mix thoroughly. Chill before serving.

Entire recipe makes 4 servings.

<u>Grams Of Fat Per Serving</u>　　　<u>Calories Per Serving</u>
　　　less than 1　　　　　　　　　　　145

Ultra Low Fat

VEGETABLE POCKETS

6 egg roll wrappers
1 cup cabbage, sliced
1 cup broccoli, chopped
1/2 cup onion, sliced
1 cup carrots, sliced
2 egg whites, slightly beaten
1/2 t. salt
1 cup *Alpine Lace Free & Lean* fat free cheese, shredded
Dash seasoned salt
Molly McButter and black pepper to taste

Preheat oven: 375°
Precook vegetables in a small amount of water; season with black pepper, salt, and Molly McButter. Cook in microwave or on range top. Cook until tender. Drain and cool vegetables.

Dip one side of egg roll wrapper in egg white. Dipped side is outside of pocket. Place approximately 1/2 cup of vegetables in center of egg roll wrapper, sprinkle about 2 T. cheese on top of vegetables, and fold wrapper to make a triangle. Seal with egg white. Repeat for remaining vegetables and wrappers. Place on baking sheet sprayed with non-stick cooking spray. Bake at 375 degrees for 14-20 minutes or until golden brown.

Entire recipe makes 6 servings.

Grams Of Fat Per Serving   Calories Per Serving
1   153

Ultra Low Fat

SUMMER RICE SALAD

Salad:

4 cups cooked rice
2 green onions, chopped
1/2 red sweet pepper, chopped
1/2 green sweet pepper, chopped
2 stalks celery, chopped
1 cup water-packed artichokes, drained
1 cup canned corn, drained
1/2 t. salt

Dressing:

1 cup fat free Italian dressing
1 1/2 t. dry ranch dressing mix
2 T. chopped onion

In large bowl, combine all ingredients for salad. Set aside.
Place all ingredients for dressing in food processor or blender and mix until onion is pureed. Pour dressing over salad and toss. Chill for 2-3 hours before serving.

Entire recipe makes 8 servings.

Grams Of Fat Per Serving   Calories Per Serving
        less than 1   164

Ultra Low Fat

CHEESY ARTICHOKE BAKE

2 14 oz. cans artichoke hearts (water packed)
1 cup *Alpine Lace Free & Lean* fat free cheese, shredded
4 T. lite sour cream
2 t. lemon juice
1/2 t. garlic powder
1/4 cup fat free mayonnaise
1/4 cup water
1 T. grated onion

Preheat oven: 350°

Spray 8" square baking dish with non-stick cooking spray. Line bottom of dish with artichoke hearts. In small bowl, mix together lite sour cream, lemon juice, garlic powder, fat free mayonnaise, onion and water. Pour this mixture over artichokes. Cover top with shredded cheese. Bake in 350 degree oven 25-30 minutes.

Entire recipe makes 6 servings.

Grams Of Fat Per Serving
less than 1

Calories Per Serving
115

Ultra Low Fat

CREAMY SKILLET POTATOES

4 medium potatoes, peeled and cubed
1/3 cup onion, chopped
1 1 oz. package ranch dressing mix
4 T. lite sour cream
2 cups skim milk
1/2 t. parsley

Precook potatoes in microwave until slightly tender. Spray large skillet with non-stick cooking spray. Brown onions and potatoes. When potatoes are golden brown, add all remaining ingredients and simmer until sauce thickens. Serve warm. Great side dish with almost any meal.

Entire recipe makes 6 servings.

Grams Of Fat Per Serving   Calories Per Serving
        less than 1   114

Fat Free

BAKED SUMMER SQUASH
WITH CHEESE

4 cups fresh yellow crookneck squash, sliced
16 fat free saltines, crushed
1 cup *Alpine Lace Free & Lean* fat free cheese,
shredded
1/4 cup onion, chopped
1/2 cup canned evaporated skim milk (0 gms. fat)
1/4 t. Molly McButter
1/2 t. salt
Black pepper to taste

Preheat oven: 350°

Cook sliced squash in microwave with 1/4 cup water
until tender. Spray 9" square baking dish with non-
stick cooking spray. Use half the precooked squash
and place over the bottom of the dish. Add a layer
of onion, and half the shredded cheese. Add the
remaining squash and another layer of cheese. In
small bowl mix together milk, salt, Molly McButter
and black pepper. Pour this mixture over casserole.
Add cracker crumbs on top and bake at 350 degrees
for 20-25 minutes.

Entire recipe makes 6 servings.

Grams Of Fat Per Serving   Calories Per Serving
0   107

RANCH STYLE GREEN BEANS

2 16 oz. cans French cut green beans, drained
1/2 cup onion, chopped
6 slices turkey bacon, already cooked and crumbled
3/4 cup canned evaporated skim milk
1 1 oz. pkg. ranch salad dressing mix
16 fat free saltines, crushed
1 cup *Alpine Lace Free & Lean* fat free cheese, shredded
1/4 cup water

Preheat oven: 350°

In small bowl, mix together, milk, ranch dressing mix, and water. Set aside. Spray 11' X 7" casserole dish with non-stick cooking spray. Spread 1 can of green beans on bottom of casserole. Sprinkle crumbled turkey bacon over green beans. Add a layer of chopped onion. Add another layer of green beans and place shredded cheese in a layer over the green beans. Pour milk and dressing mixture over entire casserole. Top with crushed crackers. Bake at 350 degrees for 20-25 minutes or until browned.

Entire recipe makes 6 servings.

Grams Of Fat Per Serving	Calories Per Serving
2	144

POTATOES AU GRATIN

4 medium potatoes sliced 1/4" thick
1 10 oz. can Weight Watchers cream of mushroom soup
4 T. lite sour cream
1 medium onion, chopped
1 cup *Alpine Lace Free & Lean* fat free cheese, shredded
Salt and black pepper to taste

Preheat oven: 375°

Arrange sliced potatoes and onions in large casserole dish sprayed with non-stick cooking spray. In small mixing bowl, combine soup with lite sour cream. Use a hand beater to mix it well. Add salt and pepper and pour mixture over potatoes. Sprinkle cheese on top. Bake covered at 375 degrees for 1 hour.

Entire recipe makes 6 servings.

Grams Of Fat Per Serving
1

Calories Per Serving
147

Fat Free

OVEN FRIED POTATOES

2 medium potatoes, peeled and sliced 1/4" thick
Butter flavored non-stick cooking spray
Seasoned salt
Black pepper to taste
1/4 cup water

Cook sliced potatoes in microwave with 1/4 cup water for approximately 5 minutes. Remove and cool slightly. Spray a baking sheet with non-stick cooking spray. Spread potatoes on baking sheet and sprinkle with seasoned salt and pepper. Spray potatoes lightly with non-stick cooking spray and place under broiler for a few minutes until brown on one side. Be careful; these burn quickly. Remove from broiler. Turn potatoes and brown on the other side. Serve.

Entire recipe makes 2 servings.

Grams Of Fat Per Serving   Calories Per Serving
              0   110

CREAM OF POTATO SOUP WITH CHEESE

1 large potato, peeled and diced
1 1/2 cup skim milk
1 cup canned evaporated skim milk
1 t. dry onion flakes
2 T. lite sour cream
1/2 t. salt
1/2 t. celery flakes
1/2 cup *Alpine Lace Free & Lean* fat free cheese, shredded (for garnish)
Black pepper to taste
Dash of seasoned salt

Combine all ingredients, except cheese, in medium sauce pan and simmer over very low heat for 15-20 minutes or until potatoes are done. When ready to serve, garnish top of each bowl of soup with shredded cheese.

Entire recipe makes 4 servings.

Grams Of Fat Per Serving | Calories Per Serving
less than 1 | 108

GUILT FREE POTATO SALAD

2 potatoes, cooked
2 green onions sliced thin
1 stalk celery chopped
I egg white from hard boiled egg, chopped (dispose of yolk)
4-5 T. fat free mayonnaise
1/2 t. lemon juice
1 t. prepared mustard
1/2 t. celery seed, if desired
1 T. sweet pickle relish, if desired
Salt and pepper to taste
Add a little green pepper or pimento if desired

Chop potato into small chunks. Add other chopped vegetables and egg. In small bowl mix fat free mayonnaise with mustard and lemon juice. Add 2-3 T. of water to thin mix and pour over potatoes. Stir and mix gently. Add any remaining ingredients to your taste. Mix. Best served after salad has been stored in refrigerator overnight or all day so the potatoes will absorb the flavors.

Entire recipe makes 4 servings.

Grams Of Fat Per Serving | Calories Per Serving
0 | 82

GREEN CHILE CHEESE SOUP

4 cups tomato juice
1 4 oz. can, chopped green chilies
1/4 cup onion, chopped fine
1 clove garlic, crushed
1/3 cup *Alpine Lace Free & Lean* fat free cheese, shredded
Dash of tabasco sauce
Dash of seasoned salt

Garnish if desired with: Chopped parsley and sprinkles of fat free cheese

Heat tomato juice in medium sized saucepan. Add all remaining ingredients and simmer over low heat until cheese is melted. Stir constantly. Serve hot and garnish with a little chopped parsley and a sprinkle of fat free cheese.

Entire recipe makes 4 servings.

Grams Of Fat Per Serving
0

Calories Per Serving
72

RED WINE GARLIC POTATOES

2 medium potatoes, peeled and cut into small chunks
1/4 cup water
1 t. dry onion flakes
1/4 t. parsley
3 T. fat free mayonnaise
1/8 t. salt
Garlic flavored red wine vinegar

Cover and cook potatoes in microwave with 1/4 cup water. Cook about 4-5 minutes, or until potatoes are tender. Do not overcook. Let stand, covered, 2-3 minutes after removing from microwave. Pour off any remaining water and sprinkle potatoes generously with garlic flavored vinegar. Add onion and stir. Allow the potatoes to cool for 5 minutes and then add fat free mayonnaise, salt, parsley. Stir gently. Serve hot or cold.

Entire recipe makes 2 servings.

Grams Of Fat Per Serving   Calories Per Serving
0   118

Ultra Low Fat

MEXICAN TOSSED SALAD

3 cups fresh lettuce
1/2 cup fresh spinach
2 radishes, sliced
1 tomato, chopped
1 small purple onion, chopped
1 jalapeno pepper, sliced (use green chile for milder taste)
1/2 cup *Alpine Lace Free & Lean* fat free cheese, shredded
1 t. cilantro

Dressing:

1 cup chunky salsa
2 T. lite sour cream

Combine all ingredients for salad in large bowl and toss gently. In small bowl, combine dressing ingredients and mix. Pour dressing over salad just before serving.

Entire recipe makes 4 servings.

Grams Of Fat Per Serving   Calories Per Serving
   less than 1   72

SALAD SANDWICH

2 slices fat free bread
2 T. fat free mayonnaise
Salt and black pepper to taste
Any of the following vegetables, stacked on bread to
make a nice thick sandwich:

Tomato
Cucumber
Sprouts
Onion
Cabbage
Lettuce
Mushrooms
Sspinach
Artichoke hearts (not marinated in oil)
Radish
Grated carrot

Spread fat free mayonnaise on each slice of bread
and stack on any vegetables to make a salad
sandwich. Note: Do not use avocado, as it is too
high in fat.

Entire recipe makes 1 serving.

Grams Of Fat Per Serving	Calories Per Serving
0	164

SWEET POTATOES WITH PINEAPPLE

2 fresh sweet potatoes, peeled and sliced (1/4 ")
1 8 oz. can pineapple tidbits (save juice)
1 T. brown sugar
1/4 t. Molly McButter
1 T. water

Preheat oven: 350°

In small bowl, combine juice from canned pineapple, water, brown sugar and Molly McButter. Mix until sugar is dissolved. In medium sized bowl, combine sweet potatoes, pineapple and pineapple juice mixture. Pour into small casserole dish sprayed with non-stick cooking spray. Bake at 350 degrees for 35 to 40 minutes or until potatoes are tender.

For variation see page 171.

Entire recipe makes 4 servings.

Grams Of Fat Per Serving | Calories Per Serving
0 | 143

STUFFED BAKED ONIONS

4 large sweet onions
3 1/2 cups boxed stuffing mix (must contain 1 gm. of fat per serving for mix only)
2 stalks celery, chopped fine
2 cups chicken broth (use canned and remove fat from top)
4 T. lite sour cream
1 egg white, slightly beaten
Salt to taste
Black pepper to taste

Preheat oven: 350°

Remove centers of onion, leaving enough outside shell to stand alone after center is removed. To remove centers, cut top and bottom from onion and carefully remove several inside layers from the onion, starting with the center and working out. Save enough of the onion centers to provide 1/2 cup chopped onion to mix with stuffing.

Brown chopped onion and celery in skillet sprayed with non-stick cooking spray. Set aside to cool slightly. In large bowl combine stuffing mix, browned onion and celery, salt and pepper and egg white. Fill each onion with stuffing mix.

In small bowl stir lite sour cream until creamy. Gradually add chicken broth and stir until all chicken broth is added. Place stuffed onions in baking dish sprayed with non-stick cooking spray. Pour a small amount of cream sauce over each stuffed onion and pour the rest of the sauce in the bottom of the baking dish. Bake uncovered at 350 degrees for 35-40 minutes or until onions are tender. Serve as a side dish with meat if desired.

Entire recipe makes 4 servings.

Grams Of Fat Per Serving   Calories Per Serving
             3   264

MANDARIN ORANGE SALAD WITH SOUR CREAM DRESSING

1 11 oz. can mandarin orange slices, drained
1 cup green seedless grapes
1 cup red seedless grapes
1 cup pineapple tidbits, save juice
4 T. lite sour cream
1 T. sugar

In large bowl, combine fruit. In small bowl combine juice from pineapple, lite sour cream and sugar. Stir until sugar is dissolved. Pour this mixture over fruit and chill at least 1 hour before serving.

Entire recipe makes 6 servings.

Grams Of Fat Per Serving
less than 1

Calories Per Serving
131

Ultra Low Fat

CHEESE POTATOES

2 large baking potatoes, peeled
4 T. lite sour cream
1/4 t. dry onion flakes
1/2 t. tabasco
1/4 t. garlic powder
2 t. lemon juice
1 cup *Alpine Lace Free & Lean* fat free cheese, shredded

Preheat oven: 350°

Cut potatoes in half and then cut each half lengthwise into 3-4 wedges. Place potato wedges into medium sized casserole sprayed with non-stick cooking spray. In small bowl combine lite sour cream, onion, tabasco, garlic powder and lemon juice. Mix together. Pour this mixture over potatoes and top with shredded cheese. Bake covered at 350 degrees for 35 minutes.

Entire recipe makes 4 servings.

Grams Of Fat Per Serving | Calories Per Serving
1 | 150

Ultra Low Fat

POTATO & ONION POCKETS

1 large potato, sliced (1/4" slices)
1 medium onion, sliced
1/3 cup water
4 T. lite sour cream
2 t. dry ranch dressing mix
1 egg white, slightly beaten
4 egg roll wrappers
Salt and black pepper to taste

Preheat oven: 375°

Cook potatoes and onions with 1/3 cup water in the microwave for 3-4 minutes or until tender. Do not overcook. Remove, drain and cool.

In small bowl, mix together the lite sour cream, ranch dressing mix. Pour this mixture over potatoes. Add salt and pepper to taste. Dip one side of the egg roll wrapper in egg white. The dipped side will be the outside of the pocket. Place about 1/2 cup of onions and potatoes in center of wrapper. Fold corner of wrapper over to meet opposite corner to form a triangle. Seal edges with egg white. Place on baking sheet, sprayed with non-stick cooking spray. Repeat for remaining wrappers. Bake at 375 degrees for 15-20 minutes or until golden brown.

Entire recipe makes 4 servings.

Grams Of Fat Per Serving	Calories Per Serving
2	133

Fat Free

PASTA SAUCE

2 cups canned tomato sauce
1 small onion, chopped
1 clove garlic, crushed
1/2 t. Italian seasoning
1/2 cup mushrooms, sliced
1/4 t. anise seed

Combine all ingredients in medium sized saucepan. Simmer over low heat for 7-8 minutes. Serve over cooked pasta. Store in refrigerator and use as needed.

Entire recipe makes 3 servings.

Grams Of Fat Per Serving
0

Calories Per Serving
72

Fat Free

RASPBERRY WINE SALAD DRESSING

1/4 cup raspberry wine
1/2 cup fat free mayonnaise
1/4 cup water
1/2 t. poppy seed
1 clove fresh garlic
1 T. chopped onion
1/4 cup white vinegar
2 t. sugar
1/8 t. salt
Pinch of dry mustard

Combine all ingredients in food processor or blender. Process until smooth. Wonderful on fresh green salad.

Chill before serving.

Entire recipe makes 6 servings.

Grams Of Fat Per Serving
0

Calories Per Serving
24

Ultra Low Fat

CRAB SALAD

9 oz. crab meat, cooked
1/4 cup green pepper
2 T. pimento, chopped
1 small onion, chopped
1/4 cup fat free mayonnaise
2 t. sugar
1 t. lime juice
1 T. fresh chopped parsley
Black pepper to taste
Dash of seasoned salt
Dash of tabasco

Combine all ingredients in medium sized bowl. Chill before serving. Looks pretty served on a lettuce leaf or use as a stuffing for tomatoes. Also a good spread for crackers or a sandwich.

Entire recipe makes 4 servings.

Grams Of Fat Per Serving
less than 1

Calories Per Serving
79

Fat Free

MACARONI SALAD

4 cups cooked macaroni
1/2 cup *Alpine Lace Free & Lean* fat free cheese, shredded
1 small onion, chopped
1/4 cup green pepper, chopped
3/4 cup celery, chopped
1 cup frozen peas
1/2 cup canned sliced mushrooms
1/2 cup grated carrot
1/2 t. celery seed

Dressing:

1 cup fat free mayonnaise
2 T. lemon juice
1 t. prepared mustard
1 t. salt
4 T. lite sour cream
Dash of garlic powder
Black pepper to taste

In large bowl combine ingredients for salad and mix. Combine ingredients for dressing in small bowl and mix. Pour dressing over salad and chill before serving.

Entire recipe makes 8 servings.

Grams Of Fat Per Serving   Calories Per Serving
1   162

SKILLET RICE AND VEGETABLES

2 cups cooked rice
1/2 cup carrots
1/2 cup frozen peas
2 green onions, chopped
1/2 cup canned chicken broth (remove fat from top)
1/2 cup celery, chopped
1/2 t. lite soy sauce
1/4 t. garlic powder
1/8 t. seasoned salt
1/4 t. onion powder
4 T. lite sour cream
Black pepper to taste

Spray large skillet with non-stick cooking spray. Add onions, celery and carrots and brown slightly over low heat. Gradually add part of chicken broth and cook to desired tenderness. Add all remaining ingredients and simmer for 3 minutes. Add remaining chicken broth and lite sour cream and simmer 1-2 more minutes. Serve.

Entire recipe makes 3 servings.

Grams Of Fat Per Serving   Calories Per Serving
1   177

Fat Free and Ultra Low Fat

MAIN DISHES & CASSEROLES

Ultra Low Fat

PINEAPPLE HAM LOAF

2 lbs. LITE ham, ground. (Choose a 2 lb. fully cooked lite ham and have the butcher grind it like hamburger)
2 egg whites, slightly beaten
8 fat free saltines crushed or 1/2 cup crushed corn flakes
3 8 oz. cans crushed pineapple, drained slightly

Prehead Oven: 350 degrees

In large bowl, mix ham, egg whites, crackers and 2 cans of crushed pineapple, reserve one can. Mix thoroughly. Place mixture in large loaf pan sprayed with non-stick cooking spray. Spread one can of crushed pineapple on the top of the loaf. Bake at 350 degrees for I hour and 10-15 minutes. Serve. This is delicious cold on sandwiches.

Entire Recipe makes 10 servings.

Grams Of Fat Per Serving   Calories Per Serving
            3   104

WESTERN STYLE CHILI

1 lb. ground turkey breast or chicken breast
1 cup tomato sauce
I pkg. chili seasoning
2 cups water
1 small onion chopped
1/4 t. garlic powder
1 cup beans (optional)
Salt to taste

Brown meat in skillet sprayed with non-stick cooking spray. Add remaining ingredients and simmer till desired thickness is acquired. Serve.

Entire recipe makes 4 servings.

Grams Of Fat Per Serving
2

Calories Per Serving
160

Ultra Low Fat

TUNA AND NOODLE BAKE

1 6 oz. can of water packed tuna
2 cups cooked fat free noodles
1 medium onion chopped
1 can chicken broth (use canned, remove fat from top)
1 1/2 cups chopped celery
1 bagel, chopped in small pieces
2 t. cornstarch
1/2 cup *Alpine Lace Free & Lean* fat free cheese, shredded
Salt and black pepper to taste

Preheat Oven: 350°

Combine all ingredients in a large bowl except the bagel. Mix well. Spray medium size casserole dish with non-stick cooking spray. Pour in mixture. Sprinkle top with fat free cheese and add chopped pieces of bagel. Bake in 350 degree oven for 30 to 40 minutes. Remove from oven and serve.

Entire recipes makes 4 servings.

Grams Of Fat Per Serving	Calories Per Serving
1	220

Ultra Low Fat

SPAGHETTI SAUCE

1 lb. ground turkey breast or chicken breast
1 8 oz. can tomato sauce
1 1\2 cups water
I medium onion chopped
1/2 cup canned mushrooms, sliced
I pkg. dry spaghetti sauce mix
1/2 t. anise seed

Brown meat and onion in skillet sprayed with non-stick cooking spray. Add remaining ingredients and simmer over low heat approximately 10 minutes. Serve over pasta.

Entire recipe makes 4 servings.

Grams Of Fat Per Serving
2

Calories Per Serving
166

CRISPY CHEESE CHICKEN

4 boneless, skinless chicken breasts
1 T. lemon juice
3/4 cup fat free mayonnaise
1/4 t. garlic powder
1 cup *Alpine Lace Free & Lean* fat free cheese, shredded
2 cups crushed corn flakes

Preheat oven: 375°

Mix lemon juice and garlic powder with fat free mayonnaise and stir until well blended. Dip and roll chicken breasts first in mayonnaise, next in grated cheese and finally in crushed corn flakes until coated well on both sides. Place coated chicken breasts on a baking sheet sprayed with non-stick cooking spray. Bake at 375 degrees for 30-35 minutes or until golden brown.

Entire recipes makes 4 servings.

Grams Of Fat Per Serving	Calories Per Serving
4	280

Ultra Low Fat

MEAT & BEAN BURRITO

1 lb. ground turkey breast or chicken breast
2 T. dry onion flakes
1 4 oz. can chopped green chilies
3 T. salsa
3 cups drained pinto beans
NOTE: *If using canned beans, make sure there is no fat added. DO NOT use canned refried beans, they have lard or fat in them. It takes 2 15.5 oz. cans of beans to equal 3 cups.*
Salt and pepper to taste
8-10 flour tortillas

Brown meat in large skillet sprayed with non-stick cooking spray. Drain beans, place in large bowl and mash with potato masher. Add onion, green chili peppers and salsa to meat as it cooking. When meat is browned, add beans. Warm tortillas in microwave for about 7-10 seconds. Serve meat and bean mixture wrapped in flour tortilla.

Entire recipe makes 8-10 servings.

Grams Of Fat Per Serving
3

Calories Per Serving
165

Ultra Low Fat

TACO MEAT

1 lb. ground turkey breast or chicken breast
I medium onion chopped
1/2 cup thick and chunky salsa
1 pkg. taco seasoning mix

Brown meat in teflon skillet sprayed with non-stick cooking spray. Add onion and brown a little longer. Add salsa and mix well. Add taco seasoning and cook to desired consistency. Serve hot, rolled in flour or corn tortilla, or chill and serve cold on top of tossed salad for a taco salad. If using meat for filling in a tortilla, add chopped lettuce and tomato and 1 T. lite sour cream.

Entire recipe makes 6 servings.

Grams Of Fat Per Serving   Calories Per Serving
             1   117

FAJITAS

4 boneless, skinless chicken breasts, cut in long strips.
1 pkg. dry fajita seasoning mix
3 large green peppers, cut in long strips
3 large white onions, sliced
5 small soft flour tortillas

<u>Extras that you may want for topping</u>:
Alpine Lace Free & Lean fat free cheese
Salsa
Chopped tomato
Lettuce
Lite sour cream

You will use half the package of fajita seasoning mix
on the meat and half in the green peppers and
onions. Spray a large skillet with non-stick cooking
spray. Brown and simmer onions and green peppers
over low heat, stirring frequently for 15-20 min.
Sprinkle half the seasoning mix on the peppers and
onions. Be sure to cover with a lid. The onions will
scorch or burn easily if you're not careful. Add
about 1/4 cup water if the skillet becomes dry. The
meat has a better flavor if cooked on a charcoal grill,
but may be cooked in a skillet or under the broiler.
Before heating the grill, spray grill with non-stick
cooking spray so the meat will not stick. Cut

chicken breast in long strips. Place chicken pieces on grill and sprinkle with fajita seasoning. Cook 1 1/2 minutes on each side. DO NOT OVER-COOK. Serve chicken strips rolled in flour tortilla along with peppers and onions and any of the suggested extras you might like to add. Enjoy!

Entire recipe makes 5 servings.

Grams Of Fat Per Serving	Calories Per Serving
3	234

Ultra Low Fat

MEAT LOAF

2 lbs. ground turkey breast or chicken breast
2 egg whites
1/2 cup tomato sauce
2 T. dry chopped onion flakes
1/2 t. garlic powder
1 T. dry green pepper flakes
Salt and black pepper to taste
2 t. Worcestershire

Preheat oven: 350°

Mix all ingredients in large bowl. Place in loaf pan sprayed with non-stick cooking spray. Bake in 350 degree oven for I hour. Remove and serve. Great with a baked potato or cold on a sandwich.

Entire recipe makes 8 servings.

Grams Of Fat Per Serving   Calories Per Serving
2   143

MINI PIZZA

6 English muffins, sliced in half
I 14 oz. jar all natural pizza sauce
1 lb. ground turkey breast
1 medium onion, chopped
1 t. caraway seeds
1 cup *Alpine Lace Free & Lean* fat free cheese, shredded
1/2 t. anise seed

Spray skillet with non-stick cooking spray and brown turkey sausage. While browning meat add onion, caraway seed, anise seed and simmer 7-8 minutes. Set aside.

Spray baking sheet with non-stick spray. Lightly toast open muffin halves under broiler. After toasting the muffins lightly, remove from broiler and spoon 1 T. pizza sauce on each muffin. Spread sauce to cover entire top of muffin. Add 2-3 T. cooked meat mixture, a little more pizza sauce and fat free cheese. Place back under broiler and heat until crispy. Be careful. These burn easily. Enjoy.

Entire recipe makes 12 servings.

Grams Of Fat Per Serving	Calories Per Serving
2	179

Fat Free

PIMENTO CHEESE SPREAD

1 cup *Alpine Lace Free & Lean* fat free cheese, shredded
3 T. fat free mayonnaise
1 T. chopped pimento
2-3 T. chopped onion

Combine all ingredients in small bowl. Stir until thoroughly mixed. Spread on fat free bread for a totally fat free sandwich.

Entire recipe makes 2 servings.

<u>Grams Of Fat Per Serving</u>   <u>Calories Per Serving</u>
0   167

Ultra Low Fat

SAUSAGE & CHEESE
BREAKFAST CASSEROLE

1 1/2 cups lite pancake mix
1 1/3 cups water
1 1/2 cups *Alpine Lace Free & Lean* fat free cheese, shredded
1 lb. ground turkey sausage,
2/3 cup lite sour cream
1/4 cup water (to thin sour cream)
Salt and black pepper to taste

Preheat oven: 350°
Brown turkey sausage in large skillet sprayed with non-stick cooking spray. In medium sized bowl, combine pancake mix with 1 1/3 cups water and mix. Spray large glass baking dish (approximately 7" X 11") with non-stick cooking spray. Pour just enough pancake batter to cover the bottom of the dish. Save the remainder of the batter to pour over the top. After, covering the bottom of the dish with batter, add a layer of cooked turkey sausage and season with salt and pepper. In small bowl, thin lite sour cream with 1/4 cup water and mix. Pour this mixture over the meat. Add a layer of shredded cheese and then cover entire top with remaining pancake batter. Bake at 350 degrees for 50 minutes. Serve warm. When cutting the warm casserole, it may look sticky in the middle and appear not done, but this is just the melted cheese and sour cream. As it cools, it will set up and be more solid. Save any remaining portions and refrigerate or freeze for another meal. Just heat in the microwave.
Entire recipe makes 12 servings.

Grams Of Fat Per Serving	Calories Per Serving
6	154

MACARONI AND CHEESE

2 cups uncooked macaroni
2 cups *Alpine Lace Free & Lean* fat free cheese,
shredded
4 T. lite sour cream
1 cup chicken broth (use canned and remove fat on
top)
1/4 cup fat free mayonnaise
Dash of seasoned salt

Preheat oven: 350°

Cook macaroni as per package directions. Drain,
rinse and set aside. Mix together in small mixing
bowl, lite sour cream and fat free mayonnaise. Very
gradually add small amounts of chicken broth,
stirring constantly. Do not add all the chicken broth
at once or the mixture will be lumpy. After mixing in
all the broth, transfer mixture to small saucepan and
bring almost to a boil, stirring constantly. Add 1 1/2
cups of cheese (reserve 1/2 cup for top) and stir
mixture until cheese is melted. Add seasoned salt.
In large bowl, combine cooked macaroni with sauce
and mix. Pour into medium sized casserole sprayed
with non-stick cooking spray. Sprinkle top with
remaining cheese and bake covered in 350 degree
oven for 20-25 minutes.

Entire recipe makes 6 servings.

Grams Of Fat Per Serving   Calories Per Serving
    less than 1   170

Ultra Low Fat

LAYERED RICE AND CHEESE CASSEROLE

1 1/4 cup uncooked rice
1 lb. ground turkey breast or chicken breast
3 slices turkey bacon, cooked
2 cups fat free chicken broth (use canned and remove fat from top)
1 cup tomato sauce
1 medium onion, chopped
1 can corn, drained
1 cup *Alpine Lace Free & Lean* fat free cheese, shredded
3/4 cup green pepper, chopped
1/4 t. garlic powder
Salt and black pepper to taste
Dash of seasoned salt

Preheat oven: 350°

Brown turkey and onion in skillet sprayed with non-stick cooking spray. Add seasonings to meat and onions. Set aside. Spray a large deep casserole dish with non-stick cooking spray. Pour rice in the bottom, then make a layer of corn, another layer of green pepper, another layer of cheese, and the last layer is ground turkey or chicken breast with onions. Place the strips of bacon on top. In medium sized bowl combine chicken broth, tomato sauce, and mix. Pour this mixture over casserole. Bake covered in 350 degree oven for 1 hour, 10 minutes.

Entire recipe makes 6 servings.

Grams Of Fat Per Serving	Calories Per Serving
2	185

OLD FASHIONED CHICKEN & DUMPLINGS

Dumplings:
1 cup flour
3 egg whites
1/2 cup 1% cottage cheese
1/8 cup water
Pinch of salt

Chicken With Broth For Dumplings:
4 boneless, skinless chicken breasts, cut in chunks
2 14 oz. cans chicken broth (use canned and remove fat from top)
3 cups water
1 medium onion, chopped
1/4 t. garlic powder
1/2 cup celery, chopped fine
1/4 t. poultry seasoning
1 t. parsley
Salt and black pepper to taste

To Prepare Chicken with Broth: Spray large pot with non-stick cooking spray. Add chicken pieces and brown. Add chicken broth, water and all ingredients for broth. Simmer 30 minutes over low heat, uncovered.

To Prepare Dumplings: Beat combined egg whites and cottage cheese with mixer. Add water and salt and mix well. Add half the flour and mix by hand, mix well and add remaining flour and mix.

To Cook Dumplings: Bring chicken broth to a rolling boil. Using a tablespoon of dough at a time, drop dumplings into boiling stock. After all dough has been dropped in, reduce heat, cover and cook for 15 minutes. If a thicker, richer broth is desired, uncover and cook longer. Serve sprinkled with Molly McButter.

Entire recipe makes 8 servings.

Grams Of Fat Per Serving   Calories Per Serving
      less than 1   141

CHICKEN CROQUETTES WITH BROWN SAUCE

4 cooked, boneless, skinless chicken breasts, chopped very fine.
2 egg whites, slightly beaten
2 t. dry onion flakes
1 t. celery flakes
1/2 cup *Alpine Lace Free & Lean* fat free cheese, shredded
24 fat free saltines, ground or crushed very fine.(1/4-1/2 cup   mixed in with the croquettes, save the rest for coating)
Dash of black pepper
Dash of salt
1 T. Water

Brown Sauce:
1 1/2 T. flour
1/2 cup canned evaporated skim milk
1/2 t. salt
1/2 cup chicken broth (use canned and remove fat from top)

Preheat oven: 350°
In medium sized mixing bowl, combine all ingredients for croquettes except cracker crumbs. Stir and mix well.   Add enough cracker crumbs to absorb moisture (1/4 - 1/2 cup). Divide mixture into 4 equal parts. Shape each portion into a cone shape. Roll in

cracker crumbs and place in small baking pan, sprayed with non-stick cooking spray. Bake at 350 degrees for 35-40 minutes.

To Prepare Brown Sauce:
Spray small saucepan with non-stick cooking spray. Add flour and brown over medium heat. Stir and watch carefully as the flour will burn easily. When flour is browned, remove from heat and gradually add enough chicken broth to make a thin paste, return to heat and immediately begin add more chicken broth stirring constantly. Add milk and continue stirring and cooking until mixture thickens. Add salt and stir. When ready to serve, pour about 1/4 cup of sauce over each croquette.

Entire recipe makes 6 servings.

Grams Of Fat Per Serving
1

Calories Per Serving
180

SAUERKRAUT & MEATBALLS

Meatballs:
1 lb. ground turkey breast or chicken breast
2 egg whites, slightly beaten
4 fat free saltines, crushed fine
1 T. barley
1 clove crushed garlic

Cabbage & Kraut:
1 small head of cabbage, sliced
1 large onion, chopped
2 heaping T. barley
2 cups tomato juice
1 16 oz. can of sauerkraut
Water

In large mixing bowl, combine ingredients for meat balls and mix well. Form into walnut sized meatballs and set aside. In large pot, start layering with a layer of cabbage on the bottom, then some onion, then some meatballs and then some sauerkraut and a little barley. Repeat layers until all ingredients are used. Pour tomato juice over top and add enough water to cover the cabbage. Simmer covered for 30 minutes.

Entire recipe makes 8 servings.

Grams Of Fat Per Serving	Calories Per Serving
1	125

Ultra Low Fat

EASY & DELICIOUS BAKED FISH OR CHICKEN

4 boneless, skinless, chicken breasts
OR
4 3 oz. fish fillets
Butter flavored non-stick cooking spray
Lemon pepper
Seasoned salt

Spray baking sheet or pan with non-stick cooking spray. Place meat on pan and season with lemon pepper and seasoned salt. Spray meat lightly with non-stick cooking spray. Bake under broiler for 6 minutes. Remove from broiler and turn meat over. Season the other side with same seasonings and spray lightly with non-stick cooking spray. Return to broiler and cook another 6 minutes. Remove and serve. Goes well with rice.

Entire recipe makes 4 servings.

Grams Of Fat Per Serving	Calories Per Serving
2	125

TACO STUFFED CORNBREAD

Taco Filling:
1 lb. ground turkey breast or chicken breast
1 pkg. taco seasoning
1/3 cup water

Other Ingredients For Layers:
1 large onion, chopped
1 cup *Alpine Lace Free & Lean* fat free cheese, shredded

Cornbread:
2 1/2 cups yellow cornmeal
2 1/2 cups low fat buttermilk
2 T. sugar
1/2 t. salt
3/4 t. baking soda
1 T. baking powder
2 egg whites, slightly beaten

Preheat oven: 400°

Brown ground turkey or chicken in skillet sprayed with non-stick cooking spray. Add water and taco seasoning and simmer until all liquid is absorbed. Set aside. In large mixing bowl, combine all dry ingredients for cornbread and mix well. In small bowl, combine egg whites and buttermilk and mix. Add buttermilk mixture to dry ingredients and stir. Stir only long enough to mix ingredients well.

Use a baking pan or glass baking dish, approximately 12" X 7" sprayed with non-stick cooking spray. Pour half of cornbread batter over bottom evenly. Now add all the taco meat, sprinkled evenly for the next layer. Add a layer of fresh chopped onion and then a layer of shredded cheese. Pour the remaining cornbread batter evenly over the top. Bake at 400 degrees for 30 to 35 minutes. Cornbread will not brown on top unless it is sprayed with a little non-stick cooking spray 10 to 15 minutes before it is done. Spray lightly.

Entire recipe makes 10 servings.

Grams Of Fat Per Serving
2

Calories Per Serving
254

PELMINI
(Russian Meat Filled Dumpling)

Meat Filling:
1 lb. ground turkey breast or chicken breast
1/2 small onion, chopped very fine
1/4 t. garlic powder
Salt and black pepper to taste
Dumpling:
2 cups flour
1 egg white, slightly beaten
3/4 cup water
1 t. salt
Broth For Boiling Dumpling:
2 14 oz. cans chicken broth (use canned and remove fat from top)
3 cups water
Garnish When Served:
White vinegar
1 T. lite sour cream per serving

In medium sized bowl, combine ingredients for filling and mix well and set aside. In large bowl, combine flour and salt and mix. Add small amounts of water to flour and begin to mix, add egg white, continue adding water and mix. After mixing thoroughly, turn dough out on floured surface and kneed for 5-7 minutes. Take about 1/4 of the ball of dough and roll out to about 1/4" thick. Using a cup or glass cut circles out of the dough. Place a spoonful of the raw meat filling in the center of the circle. Fold dough in a half moon to cover the ball of meat and pinch the edges closed all the way around the half

126

moon to seal dumpling closed. Set aside and repeat process until all meat is used. Before all dumplings are made, put the broth on to boil in large pot. When all dumplings are made and broth is boiling, drop about 8 dumplings in at a time to cook. They will sink to the bottom. When the dumplings are done, they will rise to the top of the broth. Sometimes it is necessary to use a spoon and gently move dumplings around to make sure they are not sticking to the bottom of the pan. Repeat process for remaining dumplings.

Serve hot in soup bowls with a small amount of broth. About 5 dumplings is a serving. Sprinkle about a teaspoon of vinegar over each serving and garnish with 1 T. lite sour cream. Enjoy.

Entire recipe makes about 8 servings.

Grams Of Fat Per Serving	Calories Per Serving
2	189

MEAT & CHEESE RAVIOLI

<u>Meat & Cheese Filling</u>:
1 lb. ground turkey breast or chicken breast
1 cup *Alpine Lace Free & Lean* fat free cheese, shredded
3/4 t. salt
1/4 cup onion, chopped fine
1/4 t. italian seasoning
1/4 t. anise seed
Dash of seasoned salt

<u>Ravioli Dough</u>:
2 cups flour
1 egg white, slightly beaten
3/4 cup water
1 t. salt

<u>Sauce For Serving</u>:
1 16 oz. jar low fat spaghetti sauce

In medium sized bowl, combine ingredients for meat and cheese filling, mix thoroughly and set aside.

Combine ingredients for dough and mix. Place dough on floured surface and kneed for 5-7 minutes. Roll out dough on floured surface with rolling pin. Roll to about 1/4" thick. If you have a ravioli maker, they work great....Otherwise, cut small round discs in the dough with a small glass or small biscuit cutter or cookie cutter. Start a large pot about half full of water to boil. Place a small ball of meat and cheese mixture in center of circle of dough. Fold circle of dough to make a half moon and pinch all the edges firmly to seal. Set aside and repeat until all meat is used.

Drop each filled ravioli into rapidly boiling water, about 10-12 in one pot. Reduce heat and simmer for 10 minutes. Gently remove cooked ravioli from water. Pour spaghetti sauce over ravioli when served.

Entire recipe makes 8 servings.

Grams Of Fat Per Serving	Calories Per Serving
2	213

Ultra Low Fat

BARBECUE CHICKEN BAKE

4 3 oz. boneless, skinless chicken breasts
1 1/2 cups barbecue sauce (read the label, choose
one with no fat)
3 large white onions sliced
1 15 oz. can pinto beans (must be plain beans, no
fat added) drain the juice from the beans

Preheat Oven: 350°

Brown chicken on the charcoal grill or in a skillet
sprayed with non-stick cooking spray. Just sear or
seal the meat, it does not have to be cooked all the
way through, as it will bake for an hour in the oven.
Use half of the barbecue sauce and cover the bottom
of a medium sized baking dish with the sauce. Place
the browned chicken breasts over the bottom of the
dish. Cover the chicken breasts with large slices of
onion. Sprinkle the beans on top on the sliced
onions. Pour remaining barbecue sauce evenly over
the entire contents of casserole. Bake uncovered in
350 degree oven for 1 hour. Remove and serve.

Entire recipe makes 6 servings.

Grams Of Fat Per Serving	Calories Per Serving
1	218

Ultra Low Fat

OVEN FRIED CHICKEN

4 Boneless, skinless chicken breasts
2 egg whites, slightly beaten
1/2 cup crushed corn flakes
Salt and pepper to taste
Any other seasoning that you like on fried chicken

Preheat oven: 350°

Dip chicken breasts in egg white and then roll in crushed corn flakes until coated well on both sides. Place chicken on a baking sheet sprayed with non-stick cooking spray. Bake at 350 degrees for 30 to 35 minutes.

You may want to do 8-10 chicken breasts at one time and freeze or refrigerate the rest for other meals or sandwiches. It is delicious cold.

NOTE: Fish filets may be prepared the same way.

Entire recipe makes 4 servings.

Grams Of Fat Per Serving   Calories Per Serving
              4   146

CHICKEN CHEESE ENCHILADAS

4 3 oz. boneless, skinless chicken breasts
8 soft corn tortillas
1 cup enchilada sauce
2 cups white onion, chopped
1 1/2 cups *Alpine Lace Free & Lean* fat free cheese, shredded
4 T. lite sour cream
1/4 cup fat free mayonnaise
1 1/4 cup chicken broth (use canned and remove fat on top)

Preheat oven: 375°

Cut chicken breasts in long strips and brown in skillet sprayed with non-stick cooking spray. When the chicken breasts are golden brown add onion and cook for 5-7 minutes or until onions are browned also. Remove from heat and set aside. In small mixing bowl, combine lite sour cream and fat free mayonnaise. Very gradually add chicken broth to sour cream and mayonnaise mixture, stirring constantly. Do not add broth too fast or mixture will be lumpy. When thoroughly mixed, pour into small saucepan and cook over medium heat, stirring constantly until mixture starts to boil. Add 1 cup shredded cheese and stir over heat until cheese is melted. Set aside.

corn tortilla in the enchilada sauce and make sure both sides are covered with sauce. Take tortilla out of sauce and fill with slices of chicken meat, browned onion, and a little cheese. Save some cheese for topping. Roll tortilla when filled and place in small casserole dish sprayed with non-stick cooking spray. Repeat for remaining tortillas. Pour cheese and sour cream mixture over all rolled and stuffed tortillas. Sprinkle top with remaining cheese. Cover and bake at 375 degrees for 20-25 minutes. Remove and serve. Garnish with salsa if desired.

Entire recipe makes 8 servings.

Grams Of Fat Per Serving	Calories Per Serving
2	279

ONION SMOTHERED ITALIAN CHICKEN

4 4 oz. boneless, skinless chicken breasts
1 large onion, sliced
3/4 cup fat free Italian salad dressing
1/4 cup water

Preheat oven: 350°

Pour 1/2 cup Italian dressing on both sides of chicken breasts. Cover and refrigerate for several hours or overnight. Spray large skillet with non-stick cooking spray. Brown the marinated chicken breasts on each side. Place in medium sized casserole dish sprayed with non-stick cooking spray. Cover chicken breasts with slices of onion. Pour 1/4 cup Italian dressing and 1/4 cup water over onions and chicken. Cover and bake at 350 degrees for 30-35 minutes.

Entire recipes makes 4 servings.

Grams Of Fat Per Serving	Calories Per Serving
1	159

Ultra Low Fat

BREADED OVEN RANCH CHICKEN

4 boneless, skinless chicken breasts
1 1 oz. pkg. ranch dressing mix
2 egg whites, slightly beaten
1 cup *Alpine Lace Free & Lean* fat free cheese, shredded
20 fat free saltines, crushed

Preheat oven: 350°

Spray baking sheet with non-stick cooking spray. Dip chicken breasts in egg white, then roll in shredded cheese, then roll lightly in dry ranch dressing and then roll in cracker crumbs. Place each chicken breast on baking sheet sprayed with non-stick cooking spray and bake at 350 degrees for 35-40 minutes.

Entire recipe makes 4 servings.

Grams Of Fat Per Serving   Calories Per Serving
              1   255

CHICKEN STROGANOFF

4 boneless, skinless chicken breasts, cut in strips
1/2 cup onion, chopped
1/2 t. garlic powder
1/2 of 12 oz. pkg. frozen homestyle fat free noodles

Sauce:
1 10 oz. can Weight Watchers Cream of Mushroom soup
4 T. lite sour cream
1 4 oz. can sliced mushrooms

Prepare noodles according to package directions; drain and set aside.

Brown chicken strips in skillet sprayed with non-stick cooking spray. Add garlic powder and onion and continue to brown. Simmer meat until tender. Add sauce ingredients to chicken and stir. Add noodles, or serve on top of noodles.

Entire recipe makes 4 servings.

Grams Of Fat Per Serving	Calories Per Serving
3	283

RANCH SKILLET STEW

1 lb. ground turkey breast or chicken breast
5 T. lite sour cream
1 cup skim milk
1 1 oz. pkg. ranch dressing mix
1 t. dry onion flakes
2 carrots, peeled and cut in chunks
1 large potato, peeled and cut in chunks

Cook potatoes and carrots in a small amount of water in the microwave oven until tender; drain water.

Brown meat in skillet sprayed with non-stick cooking spray. Add lite sour cream, ranch dressing mix, milk, and onion to browned meat. Stir and simmer for 1 minute. Add cooked vegetables and simmer to desired consistency.

Entire recipe makes 5 servings.

Grams Of Fat Per Serving   Calories Per Serving
2   156

Ultra Low Fat

FETTUCINE ALFREDO

1/2 of 12 oz. package of fettucine noodles
1 cup chicken broth (use canned and remove fat from the top)
1/2 cup *Alpine Lace Free & Lean* fat free mozzarella cheese
1 T. flour
1 T. onion, chopped
1/4 t. garlic powder
6 T. lite sour cream

Boil noodles according to package directions. In food processor or blender combine chicken broth, *Alpine Lace Free & Lean* fat free cheese, flour, onion, garlic powder and lite sour cream. Blend until smooth. Pour sauce into saucepan and simmer to desired thickness. This is a fairly thin sauce and will thicken somewhat when mixed with the noodles. If you desire a thicker sauce, add 1/2 - 1 T. extra flour. Pour sauce over noodles and toss lightly. Serve warm. Cooked crab or lobster could be added to make a main dish.

Entire recipe makes 6 servings.

Grams Of Fat Per Serving | Calories Per Serving
2 | 125

Ultra Low Fat

PEPPERED CAJUN CHICKEN

4 boneless, skinless chicken breasts
1 t. cajun seasoning *
Course ground black pepper
1 large onion, chopped
3 stalks celery, chopped
1 1/2 cups fresh or frozen sliced okra (not breaded)
1/2 t. salt

Preheat oven: 325°

Season each side of chicken breasts with cajun seasoning and plenty of black pepper. Brown chicken breasts in skillet sprayed with non-stick cooking spray. Cook just long enough to brown on each side. Remove chicken breasts from skillet and brown onions and celery in same skillet. Spray 9"X 9" baking dish with non-stick cooking spray. Line bottom of dish with browned onion and celery. Add okra on top of onions and celery. Add salt and a little more cajun seasoning. Place browned chicken breasts on top and cover and bake at 325 degrees for 30-35 minutes or until chicken breasts are tender.

Entire recipe makes 4 servings.

Grams Of Fat Per Serving   Calories Per Serving
              1   162

*There are several different cajun seasonings on the market. All are somewhat similar in taste. Any brand may be used.

BUTTERMILK AND CHEESE GRITS CASSEROLE

3/4 cup quick grits
3 cups buttermilk
1/4 t. Molly McButter
1/4 t. salt
1 15 oz. can corn, drained
1/3 cup chopped onion
1 cup *Alpine Lace Free & Lean* fat free cheese, shredded
1/4 t. garlic powder
2 egg whites, slightly beaten

Preheat oven: 350°

Microwave first 4 ingredients in 1 qt. microwave safe bowl. Microwave on high 4-6 minutes or until all liquid is absorbed and grits are beginning to be thick. Set aside to cool. After mixture has cooled, stir in egg white, corn, onion, garlic powder and 1/2 cup of the shredded fat free cheese. Reserve remainder of cheese for top. Pour mixture in 11"X 7" baking dish sprayed with non-stick cooking spray. Sprinkle remaining fat free cheese over the top. Bake uncovered in 350 degree oven for 25-30 minutes.

Entire recipe makes 8 servings.

Grams Of Fat Per Serving	Calories Per Serving
less than 1	138

Ultra Low Fat

CALZONES

Filling:
1 lb. ground turkey breast or chicken breast
1/2 cup onion, chopped
1/2 t. oregano
1/2 t. caraway seeds
1/3 cup fat free Italian salad dressing
1/4 t. salt
1/2 cup *Alpine Lace Free & Lean* fat free cheese, shredded
1 cup 1% cottage cheese

Crust:
6 egg roll wrappers
2 egg whites, slightly beaten

Preheat oven: 375°

Brown meat and onion in large skillet sprayed with non-stick cooking spray. Add oregano, caraway seeds, fat free italian dressing and salt. Stir and cook until meat is done. Remove from heat and add cottage cheese.

Dip one side of the egg roll wrapper in egg white. The egg white side should be the outside. Place 1/2 cup filling in the center of the wrapper and add about 1 T. fat free cheese. Fold each corner of the wrapper to the center and form a sort of package. Place on baking sheet sprayed with non-stick cooking spray and bake at 375 degrees for 20-25 minutes or until golden brown.

Entire recipe makes 6 servings.

Grams Of Fat Per Serving
2

Calories Per Serving
227

Ultra Low Fat

BARBECUE BURGER PATTIES

1 lb. ground turkey breast or chicken breast
1 T. dry onion soup mix
1/2 cup barbecue sauce
1 medium onion, chopped
Salt and black pepper to taste

Combine all ingredients in large bowl and mix. Form in **6** patties and cook in skillet sprayed with non-stick cooking spray or grill on outdoor grill. If grilling outdoors, be sure to spray grill with non-stick cooking spray <u>BEFORE</u> heating or lighting. Cook over medium to low heat about 3-4 minutes on each side.

Entire recipe makes **6** servings.

Grams Of Fat Per Serving	Calories Per Serving
1	123

LAYERED CASSEROLE

1 lb. ground turkey breast or chicken breast
3/4 cup onion, chopped
1/2 green pepper, chopped
1 cup 1% cottage cheese
1 8 oz. can tomato sauce
3 T. lite sour cream
6 T. lite cream cheese
1 t. salt
1/2 cup *Alpine Lace Free & Lean* fat free cheese
3 cups cooked pasta, drained
Black pepper to taste

Preheat oven: 350°

Brown meat and onion in large skillet spayed with non-stick cooking spray. Add tomato sauce and seasonings. Simmer 7-8 minutes. In large bowl combine green pepper, cottage cheese, cream cheese and sour cream. Mix thoroughly.

Spray large casserole dish (9" X 13") with non-stick cooking spray. Cover bottom with pasta. Add a layer of meat mixture. Pour cottage cheese mixture for next layer and top with shredded fat free cheese. Bake uncovered at 350 degrees for 30-40 minutes.

Entire recipe makes 8 servings.

Grams Of Fat Per Serving	Calories Per Serving
2	202

SHRIMP WITH SOUR CREAM TOMATO SAUCE

1 lb. cooked shrimp
1 medium onion, chopped
3/4 cup tomato sauce
1/2 cup mushrooms, sliced
2 t. lemon juice
1/4 t. garlic powder
6 T. lite sour cream
1/2 t. sesame seeds
1/4 t. lite soy sauce
1/4 t. crushed red pepper

Brown onion and sesame seeds in skillet sprayed with non-stick cooking spray. Add all remaining ingredients and simmer for five minutes. Good served over hot cooked rice.

Entire recipe makes 6 servings.

Grams Of Fat Per Serving	Calories Per Serving
2	120

FLORENTINE TURKEY LOAF WITH CHEESE

1 lb. ground turkey breast or chicken breast
2 egg whites, slightly beaten
1 medium onion, chopped fine
1 green pepper, chopped
1 cup frozen chopped spinach, thawed and drained well
1/2 t. salt
1 cup *Alpine Lace Free & Lean* fat free cheese, shredded
1/4 t. garlic powder
1 t. parsley flakes
Black pepper to taste
Few drops Worcestershire sauce

Preheat oven: 350°

Combine all ingredients in a large bowl and mix. Place in large loaf pan sprayed with non-stick cooking spray. Bake at 350 degrees for one hour. Serve warm.

Also wonderful sliced cold for sandwiches.

Entire recipe makes 8 servings

Grams Of Fat Per Serving
1

Calories Per Serving
116

Ultra Low Fat

HAM, CHICKEN AND CHEESE ROLLS

4 boneless, skinless chicken breasts
4 slices lite ham (1 gm. fat per slice)
4 slices *Alpine Lace Free & Lean* fat free cheese
4 egg roll wrappers
1 egg white, slightly beaten
1/2 cup onion, chopped
Salt and black pepper to taste

Preheat oven: 350°

Dip one side of egg roll wrapper in egg white. The dipped side should be the outside of the roll. Place one slice of ham in center of wrapper. Place chicken on top of ham. Season with salt and pepper and sprinkle on a tablespoon of chopped onion. Place one slice of fat free cheese on top of onion and start rolling wrapper with chicken and ham. Roll halfway, fold in sides and continue rolling. Place on a baking sheet sprayed with non-stick spray. Bake at 350 degrees for 35-40 minutes.

Entire recipe makes 4 servings.

Grams Of Fat Per Serving   Calories Per Serving
          3   268

146

Ultra Low Fat

LUMPIA

1/2 lb. ground turkey breast or chicken breast
4 cups cabbage, sliced
1 small onion, chopped
1/4 t. seasoned salt
1/4 t. garlic powder
1/3 cup bamboo shoots
1/3 cup water chestnuts
1/4 t. lite soy sauce
15-20 won-ton wrappers
2 egg whites, slightly beaten

Preheat oven: 375°

Brown meat in large skillet sprayed with non-stick spray. Add all chopped vegetables and seasonings and simmer, stirring occasionally for 15-20 minutes. Dip one side of won-ton wrapper in egg white. Dipped side should be the outside. Place about 1 T. of meat and vegetable mixture in the center of won-ton wrapper, and then fold like a small square package. Place on baking sheet sprayed with non-stick spray and repeat until all meat is used. Bake at 375 degrees for 10-12 minutes or until golden brown.

Entire recipe makes 4 servings.

Grams Of Fat Per Serving	Calories Per Serving
2	212

Ultra Low Fat

CHICKEN SPREAD

2 boneless, skinless chicken breasts, cooked and ground
1/2 cup onion, pureed
2 egg whites, cooked, peeled and chopped (do not use yolk)
1 stalk celery, chopped fine
1/4 t. salt
2-3 T. fat free mayonnaise
Dash garlic
Dash seasoned salt
Black pepper to taste

In food processor, grind chicken and onion together. Add salt, seasoned salt, garlic, pepper, and fat free mayonnaise. Process until mixed. Remove from processor and add celery and chopped egg whites. Stir and mix all ingredients. Serve on crackers or use as a spread for fat free bread.

Entire recipe makes 3 servings.

Grams Of Fat Per Serving   Calories Per Serving
1   122

Ultra Low Fat

STUFFED CHICKEN ROLL-UPS

4 boneless, skinless chicken breasts
4 egg roll wrappers
2 cups boxed stuffing mix (1 gm fat/serving)
2 stalks celery, chopped
1/2 cup onion, chopped
1/2 cup chicken broth (use canned and remove fat from top)
1 egg white, slightly beaten
Salt and black pepper to taste
Dash of sage

Preheat oven: 350°

Brown onion and celery in skillet sprayed with non-stick spray. In medium sized bowl combine stuffing mix, onion, celery, broth, salt, pepper, and sage. Mix.

Dip one side of egg roll wrapper in egg white. The dipped side will be the outside of the roll. Place chicken breast in center of each wrapper. Spread stuffing mixture over chicken breast and roll wrapper with chicken halfway. Fold in side corners and continue rolling. Place on a baking sheet sprayed with non-stick spray and bake at 350 degrees for 35-40 minutes or until golden brown.

Entire recipe makes 4 servings.

Grams Of Fat Per Serving	Calories Per Serving
4	432

BROILED HALIBUT FILETS
With Ranch Sour Cream

2 halibut filets
4 T. lite sour cream
2 t. lemon juice
1 1/2 t. dry ranch dressing mix

In small bowl combine lite sour cream, lemon juice and ranch dressing mix. Stir until blended. Place halibut on pan for broiling. Cover each filet with sour cream sauce. Broil 8-10 minutes. Fish is done when it flakes with a fork.

Entire recipe makes 2 servings.

Grams Of Fat Per Serving | Calories Per Serving
3 | 159

Ultra Low Fat

CORN AND HAM BAKE

6 slices lite ham (1 gm fat/slice), cut in pieces
3 cups canned whole kernel corn, drained
1/2 cup *Alpine Lace Free & Lean* fat free cheese, shredded
1 1/2 T. flour
1 cup skim milk
1/2 t. dry onion flakes
Black pepper to taste

Preheat oven: 350°

In food processor or blender, mix flour and skim milk until smooth. Remove from processor, add onion, and mix. Spray a 9" square baking dish with non-stick spray. Combine corn and lite ham and mix. Pour in baking dish. Pour milk mixture over corn and ham. Season with pepper and top with shredded cheese. Bake at 350 degrees for 30-35 minutes.

Entire recipe makes 6 servings.

Grams Of Fat Per Serving	Calories Per Serving
1	120

MARINATED SHRIMP

Seasoned Water For Boiling:
1 lb. fresh shrimp, peeled and cleaned
2 t. dry celery flakes
2 t. dry onion flakes
1 T. pickling spice
8 cups water

Marinade:
1 cup fat free Italian dressing
I medium onion, sliced
1/2 t. celery seed
2 t. green pepper flakes
2 dashes tabasco sauce

Place peeled and cleaned shrimp in 8 cups boiling water with seasonings listed above for boiling. Cook shrimp in seasoned water for 15 minutes. Let stand and cool in same water. Prepare ingredients for marinade and mix. Remove shrimp from seasoned water and arrange in shallow dish. Pour marinade over shrimp. Chill for several hours or overnight before serving.

Entire recipe makes 6 servings.

Grams Of Fat Per Serving	Calories Per Serving
1	101

Ultra Low Fat

SHRIMP & VEGETABLE PIE
With Cheese

12 oz. cooked shrimp
1/2 cup corn, drained if canned
1/2 cup carrots, sliced very thin
1/2 cup frozen peas, thawed and drained
1 8 oz. carton liquid egg substitute (must be 0 gms. fat)
1 cup skim milk
1/2 t. dry onion flakes
3 T. flour
1/2 t. salt
1 cup *Alpine Lace Free & Lean* fat free cheese, shredded
1/2 t. celery flakes
1/2 t. green pepper flakes

Preheat oven: 350°

Precook carrots for a few minutes until tender. Drain and set aside. In large bowl, combine liquid egg substitute, flour, salt, green pepper flakes, celery flakes, onion flakes, milk and mix with electric mixer. Add all vegetables and fat free cheese and stir with spoon. Spray 9" square baking dish with non-stick cooking spray. Pour mixture into baking dish and bake at 350 degrees for 40-45 minutes or until set in the center.

Entire recipe makes 8 servings.

Grams Of Fat Per Serving	Calories Per Serving
less than 1	133

TUNA AND SPINACH CASSEROLE

1 6 oz. can water packed tuna, drained
1 10 oz. pkg frozen chopped spinach, drained
1 small onion, chopped
2 egg whites, slightly beaten
4 T. lite sour cream
2 T. green pepper, chopped
1 cup *Alpine Lace Free & Lean* fat free cheese, shredded
15 fat free Saltines, crushed
1/8 t. garlic powder
Dash of seasoned salt

Preheat oven: 350°

In a large bowl, combine tuna, spinach, eggs, onion, lite sour cream, green pepper, seasoned salt, and garlic powder. Mix thoroughly. Spray 9" baking dish with non-stick cooking spray. Pour mixture into dish. Sprinkle cracker crumbs on top. Bake at 350 degrees for 30-35 minutes.

Entire recipe makes 6 servings.

Grams Of Fat Per Serving	Calories Per Serving
less than 1	134

Ultra Low Fat

HOMESTYLE NOODLES WITH CHEESE

1 12 oz. package frozen fat free homestyle noodles
1 cup *Alpine Lace Free & Lean* fat free cheese, shredded
1 cup chicken broth (use canned and remove fat from top)
1/2 t. dry onion flakes
1/2 t. celery flakes
1/2 t. salt
1/4 t. garlic powder
1/2 t. parsley flakes
1/4 t. Molly McButter
Black pepper to taste

Prepare noodles according to package directions. In medium sauce pan, combine chicken broth, onion flakes, celery flakes, salt, garlic, parsley flakes, Molly McButter and black pepper. Simmer and cook over low heat for 3-4 minutes. Add cheese to broth and stir and simmer until cheese is melted. Pour over prepared and drained noodles and serve.

Entire recipe makes 6 servings.

Grams Of Fat Per Serving
less than 1

Calories Per Serving
190

MUSHROOM SMOTHERED CHICKEN
Over Rice

4 boneless, skinless chicken breasts
1 10 oz. can Weight Watchers cream of mushroom soup
1/2 t. Molly McButter
2 cups mushrooms, sliced
1/2 t. parsley flakes
1/2 t. celery flakes
1/4 t. dry onion flakes
3 cups cooked rice
Salt to taste
Lemon pepper to taste

Season chicken breasts on both sides with lemon pepper. Brown in skillet sprayed with non-stick cooking spray. In small bowl, combine soup, Molly McButter, mushrooms, parsley flakes, celery flakes and dry onion. Mix thoroughly. Pour this mixture over browned chicken breasts in skillet and simmer about 15 minutes or until chicken breasts are tender. Serve over cooked rice.

Entire recipe makes 4 servings.

Grams Of Fat Per Serving	Calories Per Serving
2	325

Ultra Low Fat

EGG ROLLS

4 cups cabbage, sliced
1/2 cup carrot, grated
1 small onion, chopped fine
1/4 t. seasoned salt
1/8 t. black pepper
1/4 cup water
6 egg roll wrappers
2 egg whites, slightly beaten
Few drops of lite soy sauce

Preheat oven: 350°

Spray large skillet or pot with non-stick cooking spray. Brown and simmer cabbage, carrot, and onion and seasonings for 1-2 minutes. When pan becomes dry after 1-2 minutes, add water and simmer and stir until vegetables reach desired tenderness. Do not overcook. Remove from heat and cool slightly.

Dip one side of the egg roll wrapper in egg white. This will be the outside of the egg roll. Place about 1/3 to 1/2 cup of cabbage mixture just below center and roll up like an egg roll. Follow directions on the back of the egg roll wrappers if needed. Place on baking sheet sprayed with non-stick cooking spray and bake in 350 degree oven 20-25 minutes or until golden brown.

Entire recipe makes 6 servings.

Grams Of Fat Per Serving
1

Calories Per Serving
123

GREEN CHILE CHICKEN CHEESE ROLLS

4 boneless, skinless chicken breasts
4 egg roll wrappers
2 egg whites, slightly beaten
1 4 oz. can chopped green chilies
1 cup *Alpine Lace Free & Lean* fat free cheese, shredded
Salt to taste

Preheat oven: 350°

Cut chicken breasts in long strips and brown in skillet sprayed with non-stick cooking spray. Cook until almost done. The chicken will finish cooking in the oven. Dip one side of the egg roll wrapper in egg white. The dipped side will be the outside of the roll. Place about 3-4 strips of chicken just below center on the wrapper. Sprinkle on about 1-2 T. green chilies. Top with 1/4 cup shredded cheese. Season with a little salt if desired and roll up like an egg roll. Directions are on the back of the egg roll wrapper package if needed. Place rolls on baking sheet sprayed with non-stick cooking spray. and bake in 350 degree oven for 20-25 minutes or until golden brown.

Entire recipe makes 4 servings.

Grams Of Fat Per Serving	Calories Per Serving
2	282

Ultra Low Fat

GREEN CHILE QUICHE

(Makes it's own crust)

2 8 oz. cartons liquid egg substitute (Label must say 0 gms. fat)
1 4 oz. can chopped green chilies
1/2 cup 1% cottage cheese
6 T. lite sour cream
1 cup *Alpine Lace Free & Lean* fat free cheese, shredded
4 T. flour
1/4 cup onion, chopped

Preheat oven: 350°

In food processor or blender, combine eggs, cottage cheese, lite sour cream, and flour. Mix until there are no lumps remaining. Pour into large bowl, add remaining ingredients and stir. Pour into 9" pie plate sprayed with non-stick cooking spray. Bake at 350 degrees for 50 minutes.

Entire recipe makes 6 servings.

Grams Of Fat Per Serving   Calories Per Serving
            1   134

Ultra Low Fat

SHRIMP ROLLS

5 cups cabbage, sliced
1/2 cup carrots, grated
4 oz. cooked shrimp
1/4 t. seasoned salt
1/2 t. lite soy sauce
2 green onions, chopped
1/2 small green pepper, chopped
1/4 t. garlic powder
1/2 cup water
6 egg roll wrappers
2 egg whites, slightly beaten
Black pepper to taste

Preheat oven: 375°

In large pot, combine cabbage, carrots, shrimp, seasoned salt, lite soy sauce, onions, green pepper, garlic powder, black pepper and water. Simmer and stir over medium heat until vegetables are almost tender. Dip one side of the egg roll wrapper in egg white and place on dinner plate to fill. The egg white dipped side will be the outside of the roll. Use about 1/3 cup cabbage mixture for each roll. Roll like an egg roll. Directions are on the back of the package. Place on baking sheet sprayed with nonstick cooking spray. Bake at 375 degrees for 25-30 minutes or until golden brown.

Entire recipe makes 6 servings.

Grams Of Fat Per Serving
2

Calories Per Serving
150

Ultra Low Fat

CAJUN RICE & BEANS
With Onions and Cheese

3 cups cooked rice
1 15 oz. can red kidney beans
1 large onion, sliced
1 14 oz. can chicken broth (remove small amount of fat on top)
1 cup *Alpine Lace Free & Lean* fat free cheese, shredded
1/4 cup celery, chopped fine
1/2 t. cajun seasoning*
Any hot sauce to taste
Black pepper to taste

Preheat oven: 350°

Spray medium sized casserole dish with non-stick cooking spray. Layer in casserole, rice, beans, onions, celery and cheese. Season each layer with small amount of above seasonings and hot sauce. Pour chicken broth over casserole. Bake uncovered in 350 degree oven for 30-35 minutes or until most of liquid is absorbed.

Entire recipe makes 8 servings.

Grams Of Fat Per Serving   Calories Per Serving
less than 1   196

*There are several different types of cajun seasonings on the market and they all have somewhat similar tastes. Any one will work in this recipe.

SPICY MEXICAN SHRIMP

9 large shrimp, cooked
1/2 cup onion, chopped
1 fresh jalapeno pepper, sliced and seeds removed
1 cup spicy tomato juice
2 carrots, sliced
Juice of 1/2 fresh lime
1 clove garlic
1/4 t. chili powder
1/8 t. cumin
1/2 t. cilantro
1/8 t. oregano
1/4 t. salt
Dash of seasoned salt
Dash of tabasco sauce
Black pepper to taste

Brown onion in large skillet sprayed with non-stick cooking spray. Cook sliced carrots in microwave for 2-3 minutes, until slightly tender. Do not overcook. Add cooked shrimp to browned onion and add all remaining ingredients, including carrots. Simmer over very low heat for 8-10 minutes. This is great served over rice.

Entire recipe makes 3 servings.

Grams Of Fat Per Serving   Calories Per Serving
         less than 1   67

Ultra Low Fat

GREEN CHILE
ENCHILADA CASSEROLE

6 soft corn tortillas
1 lb. ground turkey breast or chicken breast, browned
1 10 oz. can enchilada sauce
1 1/2 cups *Alpine Lace Free & Lean* fat free cheese, shredded
1 cup onion, chopped
2 4 oz. cans chopped green chilies
6 T. lite sour cream
1/2 cup chicken broth (use canned and remove fat from top)
1 15 oz. can corn, drained
1 pkg. enchilada seasoning

Preheat oven: 350°
Brown meat in skillet sprayed with non-stick cooking spray. Sprinkle enchilada seasoning on the meat. Set aside. Spray 11" X 7" casserole dish with non-stick cooking spray. Line bottom and sides of dish with corn tortillas. Blend lite sour cream with chicken broth and set aside. Pour in the corn to make the first layer, then layer the green chilies, then the chopped onion and then the meat. Pour the chicken broth mixture over the casserole and then pour in the enchilada sauce. Top casserole with shredded cheese and bake at 350 degrees for 40-45 minutes.

Entire recipe makes 6 servings.

Grams Of Fat Per Serving	Calories Per Serving
2	208

CRISPY COATED BUTTERFLY SHRIMP
With Marmalade Dip

6 extra large shrimp
2 egg whites
1 1/2 cups corn flakes, crushed
Seasoned salt

Marmalade Dip:
1/2 cup orange marmalade jam
1/4 cup water
1/4 t. lite soy sauce
1/4 t. horseradish
Dash of seasoned salt

Preheat oven: 350°
Clean, de-vein and peel all shrimp. Using a sharp paring knife cut along center back of shrimp from one end to the tail. Be careful not to cut all the way through. Cut just enough to butterfly the meat. Using a standard table knife, use the handle end to gently pound the shrimp to flatten and spread it. Do not pound hard. Dip each piece in egg white and then roll in crushed corn flakes. Place on baking sheet sprayed with non-stick cooking spray. Season lightly with seasoned salt. Bake at 350 degrees for 30-35 minutes.
Just before serving, combine ingredients for dip in small sauce pan and warm over low heat. Serve with shrimp.

Entire recipe makes 2 servings.

Grams Of Fat Per Serving	Calories Per Serving
less than 1	317

Ultra Low Fat

CHICKEN MOZZARELLA

4 boneless, skinless chicken breasts
2 cups corn flakes, crushed
2 egg whites, slightly beaten
1 16 oz. jar low fat spaghetti sauce
1 cup fat free mozzarella cheese, shredded
1/4 cup water

Preheat oven: 350°

Dip chicken breasts in egg white, roll in corn flakes and place in large skillet sprayed with non-stick cooking spray. Brown on both sides. Spray a shallow baking dish with non-stick cooking spray and place chicken breasts in dish. Mix water with spaghetti sauce and pour over chicken breasts. Cover top with shredded fat free mozzarella cheese and bake at 350 degrees for 35-40 minutes.

Entire recipe makes 4 servings.

Grams Of Fat Per Serving   Calories Per Serving
4   313

Ultra Low Fat

SPICY SAUERKRAUT OVEN STEW

1 lb. ground turkey breast or chicken breast, browned
4 cups spicy tomato juice
2 medium onions, quartered
1 cup canned corn, drained
2 carrots, sliced
2 potatoes, peeled and cubed
1 16 oz. can sauerkraut, drained
1/2 t. salt
1/2 t. caraway seed
1/4 t. garlic powder
Black pepper to taste
Tabasco sauce to taste

Preheat oven: 350°

Use a large pot suitable for oven baking. Spray pot with non-stick cooking spray. Combine all ingredients. Cover and bake at 350 degrees for 1 hour or until potatoes are tender. Great with cheese toast.

Entire recipe makes 6 servings.

Grams Of Fat Per Serving
2

Calories Per Serving
189

Ultra Low Fat

CREAM OF MUSHROOM CASSEROLE

4 3 oz. boneless, skinless chicken breasts, cut in small chunks
1 12 oz. pkg. fat free homestyle frozen noodles
2 10 oz. cans Weight Watchers cream of mushroom soup
1 6 oz. can sliced mushrooms, drained.
1 t. dry onion flakes
1/2 t. dry celery flakes
1/4 t. Molly McButter
1 cup water
4 T. lite sour cream
Salt and black pepper to taste

Preheat oven: 350°

Brown chunks of chicken breast in skillet sprayed with non-stick cooking spray. Stir and turn until golden brown. Add the two cans of soup and 1 cup water. Stir until mixed well with chicken. Pour into large bowl and add remaining ingredients. When adding the frozen noodles, be sure to break them up so there are no chunks sticking together. Stir all ingredients together in bowl. Spray 11" X 7" glass casserole with non-stick cooking spray. Pour mixed ingredients into casserole and bake at 350 degrees for 1 hour. Stir the entire casserole before serving.

Recipe makes 8 servings.

Grams Of Fat Per Serving
2

Calories Per Serving
203

Ultra Low Fat

VEGETABLE PIE WITH CHEESE CRUST

1/2 of Ready Made Pizza Dough (in refrigerated biscuit section of your grocery store)
1 cup frozen chopped broccoli
1 cup corn, drained
1 1/2 cups onion, chopped
1/2 cup frozen sugar peas or Snow peas
1/2 t. garlic powder (for crust)
1 t. salt
1/4 t. seasoned salt
1/4 cup chicken broth (use canned and remove fat from top)
1/2 cup *Alpine Lace Free & Lean* fat free cheese
Black pepper to taste

Preheat oven: 350°

Remove Ready Made crust from canister and use only half the dough provided. Spray 9" pie plate with non-stick cooking spray. Use 1/2 cup shredded cheese and sprinkle cheese over dough. Press cheese into the dough with your fingers. Place dough in pie plate. Shape dough to fit bottom and edges of pie plate. Sprinkle crust with garlic powder.

Layer vegetables next and season each layer with salt, pepper and a small amount of seasoned salt. In

168

small bowl add just a few teaspoons of chicken broth to 1 1/2 T. flour. Keep adding broth to make a thin paste. Pour this mixture over vegetables and top with remaining shredded *Alpine Lace Free & Lean* fat free cheese. Bake 350 degrees for 40-45 minutes.

Entire recipe makes 8 servings.

Grams Of Fat Per Serving   Calories Per Serving
                1   141

Ultra Low Fat

SPINACH DINNER QUICHE

2 8 oz. cartons liquid egg substitute (label must say 0 gms. fat)
1/2 pkg. frozen chopped spinach
1/2 cup onion, chopped
1 cup *Alpine Lace Free & Lean* fat free cheese, shredded
1/4 t. Molly McButter
4 T. flour
6 slices turkey bacon, chopped and crumbled
Dash of seasoned salt
Dash of black pepper

Preheat oven: 350°

In food processor or blender mix eggs, Molly McButter, flour, salt and pepper. Blend only long enough so there are no lumps. In large bowl, combine all ingredients and stir. Pour into 9" pie plate sprayed with non-stick cooking spray. Bake at 350 degrees for 45 minutes.

Entire recipe makes 6 servings.

Grams Of Fat Per Serving   Calories Per Serving
            2   133

Fat Free

SCRAMBLED EGG SANDWICH

2 egg whites, or 1/2 cup fat free liquid egg substitute
1 T. onion, chopped
1 T. green pepper, chopped
1/2 t. prepared mustard
1/4 cup *Alpine Lace Free & Lean* fat free cheese, shredded
Salt and black pepper to taste
2 slices fat free bread
Fat Free mayonnaise, if desired for sandwich

In small bowl, combine egg whites and prepared mustard and beat slightly. Spray a small skillet with non-stick cooking spray. Pour egg mixture into skillet and add onions and green pepper. Stir over medium heat. Just before eggs are done, add shredded fat free cheese. Mix thoroughly. Add salt and pepper to taste. Serve on fat free bread. Spread bread with fat free mayonnaise or mustard if desired.

Entire recipe makes 1 serving.

Grams Of Fat Per Serving   Calories Per Serving
           0   195

Ultra Low Fat

MUSHROOM SOUP MEATLOAF

2 lbs. ground turkey breast or chicken breast
1 10 1/2 ounce can Weight Watchers cream of
mushroom soup
1/4 t. onion powder
1/4 t. garlic powder
1 small onion, chopped
6 fat free saltines, crushed
2 egg whites, slightly beaten
1/2 t. salt
1/4 t. black pepper
Dash of seasoned salt
Dash of tabasco sauce

Preheat oven: 350°

In large bowl combine all ingredients. Form into loaf
and place in loaf pan sprayed with non-stick cooking
spray. Bake 60-70 minutes at 350°.

Entire recipe makes 8 servings.

Grams Of Fat Per Serving	Calories Per Serving
2	155

Fat Free

CREOLE BEANS AND RICE

2 cups cooked rice
2 cups cooked or canned black or brown beans, drained
1 medium onion, chopped
1/2 cup celery, chopped
1/4 t. black pepper
1 cup tomato sauce
1/4-1/2 t. creole seasoning
1/2 t. garlic powder
5 drops tabasco sauce
1 cup sliced okra
1/2 t. worcestershire
Crushed red pepper to taste

Brown onions and celery in skillet sprayed with non-stick cooking spray. Add remaining ingredients except rice and simmer over low heat for 20 minutes. Serve over cooked rice.

Entire recipe makes 4 servings.

Grams Of Fat Per Serving   Calories Per Serving
            0   219

Ultra Low Fat

BLACK BEANS AND RICE STEW

1 16 oz. package dry black beans
1/2 cup rice
1/2 package dry onion soup mix
1/4 t. garlic powder
1/2 cup celery, chopped
2 large carrots, sliced
2 t. minced parsley
6 drops tabasco
1 cup water
3 14 1/2 oz. cans chicken broth (remove fat from top)
6 T. lite sour cream (stir in just before serving)
1/8 t. seasoned salt
Dash of seasoned salt
Black pepper to taste
Red pepper flakes to taste

Rinse beans and soak overnight. Pour water off soaked beans the next day and combine all ingredients in large pot (except for lite sour cream). Simmer over low heat for 3 1/2 to 4 hours. Add water as needed depending on how thick or thin you like your stew. Before serving, remove from heat and add lite sour cream.

Entire recipe makes 8 servings.

Grams Of Fat Per Serving
1

Calories Per Serving
234

Ultra Low Fat

GREEN CHILE ENCHILADA BAKE

2 4 oz. cans whole green chiles
1 cup fat free mozzarella cheese, shredded
1/2 cup fat free cheddar cheese, shredded
1 medium onion sliced fairly thin
1 1/2 t. packaged taco seasoning
6 soft corn tortillas
1 10 oz. can green enchilada sauce

Preheat oven: 350°

Brown onions in skillet sprayed with non-stick cooking spray. Sprinkle 1 t. taco seasoning on onions. Add a little water if they get too dry while browning. Drain canned green chiles. Warm tortillas in microwave according to package directions. Slice open each green chile and place flat and spread out on one corn tortilla. In small bowl combine cheeses. Sprinkle about 1/4 cup of mixed cheese on top of green chile. Add some browned onion slices and roll tortilla. Place in 11 x 7 casserole dish sprayed with non-stick cooking spray. Continue same procedure for the remaining tortillas and place close together in casserole dish.   Pour green sauce over the top. Sprinkle 1/2 t. taco seasoning over sauce and bake at 350° for 30-35 minutes.

Entire recipe makes 6 servings.

Grams Of Fat Per Serving
Less than 1

Calories Per Serving
148

Ultra Low Fat

HAWAIIAN CHICKEN SALAD

2 cooked, boneless, skinless chicken breasts, cut in small chunks
1 cup red seedless grapes (cut in half)
1/2 cup green seedless grapes (cut in half)
3/4 cup pineapple tidbits, drained (save juice)
1 cup celery, chopped
1 cup miniature marshmallows (add just before serving)

Dressing

1/3 cup fat free mayonnaise
1/8 cup pineapple juice
1/2 t. lemon juice

Combine all ingredients except marshmallows for salad.

In small bowl combine ingredients for dressing. Pour dressing over salad and toss. Best if chilled slightly before serving. Add marshmallows before serving.

Entire recipe makes 4 servings.

Grams Of Fat Per Serving   Calories Per Serving
1   215

Ultra Low Fat

BAKED SWEET AND SOUR CHICKEN BREASTS

8 boneless, skinless chicken breasts
1/2 cup orange marmalade
1/2 envelope onion soup mix
1/2 cup green pepper, chopped
3/4 cup orange juice
1/4 cup fat free Italian dressing
1/2 t. lite soy sauce

Preheat oven: 350°

In small bowl combine marmalade, onion soup mix, green pepper, soy sauce, orange juice and Italian dressing. Spray large pan or dish with non-stick cooking spray. Place chicken breasts on pan and pour sauce over the top. Bake at 350° for 40-45 minutes.

Entire recipe makes 8 servings.

Grams Of Fat Per Serving
1

Calories Per Serving
178

HOT AND SPICY FISH WITH CREOLE SAUCE

4 fish filets
1 6 oz. can tomato sauce
1/2 cup sliced okra
1 stalk celery, chopped
1/3 cup green pepper, chopped
1 small onion, chopped
1/2 t. red pepper flakes
1/3 cup water
1 fresh lime
Salt to taste
Spicy Cajun Seasoning for fish
Black pepper

Squeeze fresh lime juice on fish filets, then season filets on both sides very generously with cajun seasoning and black pepper. Brown in skillet sprayed with non-stick cooking spray. Combine all remaining ingredients in bowl and mix. Pour this mixture over fish filets and simmer over very low heat for 6-8 minutes.

Entire recipe makes 4 servings.

Grams Of Fat Per Serving	Calories Per Serving
1	132

CREAMED CHICKEN OVER TOASTED ENGLISH MUFFINS

1 5 oz. can chunk white chicken
1 10 1/2 oz. can Weight Watchers cream of mushroom soup
1 small onion, chopped
1 stalk of celery, chopped
1 cup frozen peas
2 English muffins, cut in half
4 slices *Alpine Lace Free & Lean* fat free cheese
Salt and black pepper to taste

Brown celery and onion in skillet sprayed with non-stick cooking spray. Add soup and simmer 2-3 minutes. Add chicken, peas and seasoning. Simmer 1-2 minutes. Toast English muffins. For each serving, place muffin half on plate and place one slice of cheese on top of muffin. Spoon hot creamed chicken over top of cheese.

Entire recipe makes 4 servings.

Grams Of Fat Per Serving   Calories Per Serving
             2   179

MEXICAN BEANS AND RICE

3 cups canned brown beans (drained)
2 cups cooked rice
1 small onion, chopped
1/3 cup chopped green chiles
3/4 cup green enchilada sauce
1 package taco seasoning
1/4 t. garlic powder
1/4 t. black pepper
1/3 cup water
1/2 cup *Alpine Lace Free & Lean* fat free cheese, shredded
Seasoned salt to taste
Crushed red pepper (if desired)

Brown onion in skillet sprayed with non-stick cooking spray. Add remaining ingredients, except rice, in skillet and simmer over very low heat for 15 minutes. Serve over cooked rice topped with shredded cheese.

Entire recipe makes 4 servings.

Grams Of Fat Per Serving   Calories Per Serving
             0   290

Ultra Low Fat

MAXINE'S COUNTRY STEW

1 lb. ground turkey breast or chicken breast
1 cup onion, chopped
1/4 cup green pepper, chopped
1 cup celery, chopped
1 cup carrots, chopped
2 cups tomatoes
8 cups water
1/4 cup barley
3 beef bouillon cubes
1/2 t. kitchen bouquet
1 cup frozen peas (added last after stew has cooked)
Salt & black pepper to taste

Combine all ingredients in large pot. Cook over low heat for 2 hours. Add peas immediately after heat is turned off while stew is still hot. Serve.

Entire recipe makes 6 servings.

Grams Of Fat Per Serving   Calories Per Serving
            1   161

Fat Free

BAKED RICE

2 cups cooked rice
2 green onions, chopped
2 egg whites, slightly beaten
1/2 cup *Alpine Lace Free & Lean* fat free cheese, shredded
1 cup canned corn, drained
1 t. lemon juice
Salt & black pepper to taste
Dash of garlic powder

Preheat oven: 350°

Combine all ingredients in large bowl. Spray round or square baking dish with non-stick cooking spray. Pour mixture in dish & bake at 350° for 25-35 minutes.

Entire recipe makes 4 servings.

Grams Of Fat Per Serving   Calories Per Serving
            0   169

Ultra Low Fat

CHICKEN BREASTS WITH GARLIC SAUCE

2 boneless, skinless chicken breasts
1/2 green pepper, sliced
1/4 red bell pepper, sliced
1 medium onion, sliced
2 T. garlic flavored wine vinegar
1 t. corn starch
1 t. sugar
1 clove garlic, crushed
1/3 cup chicken broth (fat removed)
Seasoned salt to taste
Black pepper to taste

Brown chicken breasts in skillet sprayed with non-stick cooking spray. In small bowl mix sugar, wine vinegar, garlic & chicken broth. Gradually add corn starch & mix thoroughly. Add sliced onion and bell pepper in skillet with chicken breasts. Pour liquid mixture over the top of onion and peppers and simmer about 15-20 minutes or until tender. Add salt, black pepper, and seasoned salt to taste. Serve alone or over rice.

Entire recipe makes 2 servings.

Grams Of Fat Per Serving   Calories Per Serving
2   163

SWEET POTATO CASSEROLE

1 8 oz. can pineapple tidbits, drained
1/4 cup drained juice
2 16 oz. cans sweet potatoes
1/4 t. salt
2 t. Molly McButter
1 cup miniature marshmallows
1 1/2 cups corn flakes
2 T. brown sugar

Preheat oven: 350°

In food processor combine sweet potatoes, salt, Molly McButter, and brown sugar and process. Remove mixture to bowl and fold in marshmallows and pineapple. Spread mixture in baking dish sprayed with non-stick cooking spray. Sprinkle corn flakes on top of sweet potatoes. Bake at 350° for 25 minutes.

Entire recipe makes 6 servings.

Grams Of Fat Per Serving   Calories Per Serving
            0   167

Fat Free and Ultra Low Fat

PIES, PASTRIES & DESSERTS

CHILLED ORANGE MARMALADE CREAM CHEESE PIE

<u>Crust</u>:

8 graham cracker squares, ground (square = 2 1/2"
X 2 1/2")
2 T. sugar
1 1/2 T. lite cream cheese

<u>Filling</u>:

2/3 cup orange marmalade
1/2 cup lite sour cream
1 8 oz. package or carton lite cream cheese
1/2 cup skim milk
1/2 cup boiling water
1 package unflavored gelatin
1/4 cup sugar
1/2 t. vanilla
1/4 t. salt

Mix gelatin in boiling water and stir until completely dissolved. Set aside to cool.

In food processor, combine ground graham crackers and sugar and mix. Add 1 1/2 T. lite cream cheese and process. Spray 9"-pie plate with non-stick cooking spray. Pour crust mixture into pie plate and press gently to sides and bottom to form crust. Chill.

In food processor, combine all ingredients for filling except marmalade. Process until smooth. Add gelatin water and marmalade and mix. Very gently pour filling into chilled crust. Chill pie for 3-4 hours before serving.

Entire recipe makes 8 servings.

Grams Of Fat Per Serving
2

Calories Per Serving
200

SOUR CREAM & RAISIN PUFFS

1/2 cup raisins
1/4 cup sugar
1/3 cup lite sour cream
1 T. flour
1/2 t. vanilla
1/8 t. salt
1/4 t. lemon juice
6 Won Ton wrappers
1 egg white, slightly beaten

Preheat oven: 375°

In food processor, combine lite sour cream, flour, sugar, salt, lemon juice and vanilla. Process until smooth. Pour mixture into small saucepan and stir over medium heat until mixture thickens. Remove from heat, add raisins and cool for a few minutes.

Dip one side of won ton wrapper in egg white. The dipped side will be the outside. Place about 1 heaping teaspoon of raisin and sour cream mixture in center of won ton wrapper. Bring all four corners of wrapper together at top and press lightly with fingers to seal in place. Place on baking sheet sprayed with non-stick cooking spray. Repeat for remaining wrappers. Bake at 375 degrees for
8-10 minutes or until golden brown.

Entire recipe makes 3 servings.

Grams Of Fat Per Serving	Calories Per Serving
2	215

CORN FLAKE PIE CRUST

3 cups corn flakes, crushed
2 T. sugar
1 1/2 T. lite cream cheese

Grind corn flakes in food processor, add sugar and process just enough to mix. Add half of cream cheese and process. Add remaining cream cheese and process. Spray 9" pie plate with non-stick cooking spray. Pour in crust mixture. Gently and evenly press to bottom and sides to form crust. Chill before adding filling.

Entire recipe makes 1 pie crust- about 8 servings.

Grams Of Fat Per Serving   Calories Per Serving
less than 1   45

Ultra Low Fat

BANANA MERINGUE DELIGHT

<u>Meringue Crust</u>:

3 egg whites
2 T. sugar
1/4 t. vanilla
Dash of salt
1/8 t. cream of tartar

<u>Filling</u>:

1 large 2.0 oz. package vanilla sugar-free instant pudding
3 cups skim milk
2 large bananas

<u>Topping</u>:

8 graham cracker squares, ground (square = 2 1/2" X 2 1/2")

Preheat oven: 300°

In large bowl, beat egg whites until slightly stiff. Gradually add sugar and cream of tartar and continue to beat. Add vanilla and salt and continue beating until whites stand in stiff peaks. Spray 9" X 9" glass baking dish with non-stick cooking spray. Spread meringue over entire bottom and sides of dish to form a crust. Bake in 300 degree oven for 45 minutes. Remove and cool.

After crust has cooled, prepare pudding mix according to package directions and fold in sliced bananas. Pour pudding mixture into crust and sprinkle ground graham crackers on top. Chill and serve.

NOTE: Meringue crust does not keep well over a day or two. After that it becomes soggy and tough.

Entire recipe makes 8 servings.

Grams Of Fat Per Serving   Calories Per Serving
less than 1   126

BANANA WHIP

2 bananas
2 T. sugar
1 pkg. unflavored gelatin
1 T. lemon juice
1/2 cup boiling water
2 egg whites
1/4 t. vanilla
1/2 cup maraschino cherries
Pinch of salt

Dissolve gelatin in boiling water and stir until completely dissolved.

Pour gelatin and water in food processor and add, lemon juice, sugar, and mix for one minute. Add egg whites and vanilla and mix again. Gradually add banana while mixing and continue to process until all banana is added. Add salt. Remove mixture to a large bowl and add cherries. Pour into a mold and chill several hours.

Entire recipe makes 4 servings.

Grams Of Fat Per Serving   Calories Per Serving
            0   119

Ultra Low Fat

LEMON BLINTZ PIE

3 cups 1% cottage cheese
1/3 cup liquid egg substitute (must be 0 gms. of fat)
2 egg whites
1/2 cup + 2 T. sugar
1 t. lemon juice
1 1/2 t. fresh grated lemon peel
1/4 cup lite sour cream
3 T. flour
1/8 t. salt
1 t. vanilla

Preheat oven: 325°

In food processor, combine egg whites, liquid egg substitute, sugar and vanilla. Process for 1-2 minutes. Add salt, lemon juice, lemon peel, cottage cheese, lite sour cream and flour. Process until smooth. Spray large (9") pie plate with non-stick cooking spray. Pour mixture into pie plate and bake at 325 degrees for 1 hour. Test with toothpick for doneness. If toothpick comes out clean, it is done. Center will fall as it cools. This is normal. Serve warm or cold. It is delicious either way.

Entire recipe makes 8 servings.

Grams Of Fat Per Serving   Calories Per Serving
2   156

CHOCOLATE SWIRL CHEESE CAKE

Crust:

8 graham cracker squares, ground (square = 2 1/2" X 2 1/2")
2 T. sugar

Filling:

2 8 oz. packages or cartons lite cream cheese
1 cup lite sour cream
2 egg whites
1/2 t. vanilla
1/2 cup + 2 T. sugar
1/4 t. salt
4 T. fat free chocolate ice cream topping

Preheat oven: 325°

In food processor, grind graham crackers, add sugar and mix. Spray 9" pie plate with non-stick cooking spray. Pour the graham cracker mixture into pie plate and gently spread over entire bottom of pie plate. Set aside while making filling.

In large bowl, whip egg whites with electric mixer until foamy. Add all remaining ingredients for filling and beat until smooth. Very gently pour filling mixture into pie plate on top of graham cracker mixture. Drop 1 T. of chocolate topping in four separate places on top of cheesecake. Use a table knife and cut down into the center of each drop of chocolate and drag and swirl the chocolate around the top of the cheesecake. Be careful not to cut all the way down to the crust. Repeat for each drop of chocolate. Bake at 325 degrees for 30 minutes. Reduce oven temperature to 300 degrees and bake another 35-40 minutes. Chill thoroughly before serving.

Entire recipe makes 8 servings.

Grams Of Fat Per Serving	Calories Per Serving
6	208

Ultra Low Fat

APRICOT SOUR CREAM PIE

Filling:

1 1/4 cup dried apricots
1 cup water
3 egg whites
3/4 cup sugar
1 cup lite sour cream
1 T. flour
1/2 t. salt
1 t. lemon juice
1 t. vanilla

Crust:

8 graham cracker squares, ground (square = 2 1/2"
X 2 1/2")
2 T. sugar

Preheat oven: 350°

Steam and cook apricots in 1 cup water for 10 minutes. Set aside to cool. In large bowl combine sour cream, sugar, flour, salt, lemon juice and vanilla. Beat with electric mixer until well blended. In a separate bowl, beat egg whites until stiff. Pour any remaining water off apricots and puree. Combine puree with sugar and sour cream and mix.

Spray 9" pie plate with non-stick cooking spray. Combine 2 T. sugar with graham crackers and mix. Cover the bottom of the pie plate with graham cracker mixture. Fold puree into egg whites and very gently pour this mixture into pie plate. Bake at 350 degrees for 25-30 minutes.

Entire recipe makes 8 servings.

Grams Of Fat Per Serving	Calories Per Serving
3	247

CREAM CHEESE BROWNIE CAKE

1 1/2 cups flour
1 cup sugar
1/2 t. vinegar
1/2 t. soda
1/4 cup dry cocoa
1/4 cup fat free mayonnaise
1 cup water
1/8 cup light corn syrup
1 t. vanilla
1/8 t. salt

Cream Cheese Swirl:

1/3 cup lite cream cheese
1 1/2 T. sugar
1/4 t. vanilla

Preheat oven: 350°

In large bowl, combine flour, sugar, soda, cocoa, and salt. Stir until well blended. Add water, vinegar, vanilla, fat free mayonnaise, and corn syrup and mix with electric mixer until smooth. Spray 9" baking dish with non-stick cooking spray. Pour cake batter into dish and set aside while making the cream cheese swirl.

In small bowl, combine lite cream cheese, sugar and vanilla. Mix with electric mixer until smooth and creamy. Drop about 1 T. of cream cheese mixture in four or five different places on top of the cake batter. Take a table knife and place the knife blade in the center of each cream cheese drop and drag the cream cheese with the knife through the cake. Curve and swirl the knife as you drag the cream cheese to make pretty swirls on top of the cake. Bake at 350 degrees for 40-45 minutes.

Entire recipe makes 8 servings.

Grams Of Fat Per Serving	Calories Per Serving
less than 1	232

Fat Free

OLD FASHIONED BREAD PUDDING
With Lemon Sauce

6 slices fat free bread, toasted and dried
1 cup canned evaporated skim milk
1/2 cup skim milk
1 egg white
1/4 cup sugar
1/4 cup raisins
1/4 cup liquid egg substitute (Must have 0 gms. of fat)
1/8 t. nutmeg
1/8 t. cinnamon
1/2 t. vanilla

Lemon Sauce:

1 3.4 oz. package instant sugar free lemon pudding & pie filling.
2 cups skim milk
Note: You will not need the entire recipe of pudding for 6 servings. Only 1/4 cup per serving of bread pudding.

Preheat oven: 350°

Spray small casserole dish with non-stick cooking spray. Break dried bread in small chunks and line the bottom of the casserole. Sprinkle raisins on top of bread chunks. In medium sized bowl combine evaporated milk, skim milk, egg white, sugar, liquid egg substitute, nutmeg, cinnamon and vanilla. Beat this mixture with electric mixer until well blended. Pour over chunks of bread in casserole and bake at 350 degrees for 25 to 30 minutes or until liquid is set and absorbed. Serve warm with 1/4 cup lemon sauce poured over each serving.

Entire recipe makes 6 servings.

Grams Of Fat Per Serving
less than 1

Calories Per Serving
132

LEMON CHEESECAKE

Crust:

8 graham cracker squares, ground (square = 2 1/2" X 2 1/2")
2 T. sugar

Filling:

2 8 oz. packages or cartons lite cream cheese
1 cup lite sour cream
2 egg whites
1 t. vanilla
1 1/2 t. lemon juice
1/2 t. fresh lemon peel, grated
1/2 cup + 2 T. sugar
1/4 t. salt

In food processor, grind graham crackers, add sugar and mix together. Spray 9" pie plate with non-stick cooking spray. Pour the graham cracker mixture into pie plate and gently spread over entire bottom of pie plate. Set aside while making filling.

In large bowl, whip egg whites with electric mixer until foamy. Add all remaining ingredients for filling and beat until smooth. Very gently pour filling mixture into pie plate on top of graham cracker mixture. Bake in 325 degree oven for 30 minutes. Reduce oven temperature to 300 degrees and bake another 35-40 minutes.

Entire recipe makes 8 servings.

Grams Of Fat Per Serving	Calories Per Serving
5	173

Ultra Low Fat

CHEESE BLINTZ

<u>Filling</u>:

1 cup dry curd cottage cheese
2 T. sugar
1 egg white, slightly beaten
1/2 t. vanilla
1/4 t. salt

<u>Outer Crust</u>:

4 egg roll wrappers
1 egg white, slightly beaten

Preheat oven: 375°

Drain and remove as much water as possible from the cottage cheese. In medium sized bowl, combine cottage cheese, egg white, vanilla, salt, sugar and flour. Stir and mix thoroughly. Dip one side of the egg roll wrapper in egg white and place the egg white side down on a dinner plate. Use about 1/4 cup of the cottage cheese mixture for each filling. Place the filling in a small log shaped just below the center of the egg roll wrapper. Bring the bottom corner up over the filling, bring the right and left corners to the center and then roll it forward until it forms the shape of an egg roll. Repeat same for others. Place on baking sheet sprayed with non-stick cooking spray. Sprinkle each roll with a little granulated sugar. Bake at 375 degrees for 25-27 minutes or until golden brown.

Entire recipe makes 4 servings.

Grams Of Fat Per Serving	Calories Per Serving
1	129

Fat Free

ANGEL CHOCOLATE & RASPBERRY DREAM

1/2 small angel food cake, already baked
1 large pkg.(1.3 oz.) vanilla sugar-free instant pudding
3 cups skim milk
1 cup fresh or frozen raspberries
4 T. fat free chocolate fudge topping

Use 8" square glass baking dish or similar size. Cut 1/2 of the angel food cake and cut it in half. Using 1/4 of the cake, break into bite size pieces and make a layer of cake pieces in the bottom of the dish. Sprinkle 1 cup raspberries over the pieces of cake. Prepare instant pudding according to package directions, except, beat only until mixture starts to thicken. Immediately pour half the pudding over angel food cake bits. Drizzle 2 T. chocolate fudge topping over pudding. Using the 1/4 cake that is left, break into pieces and make another layer. Pour on remaining pudding and drizzle 2 more tablespoons of chocolate fudge topping over top. Chill for at least 20 minutes before serving.

Entire recipe makes 6 servings.

Grams Of Fat Per Serving	Calories Per Serving
0	240

Ultra Low Fat

CRUNCHY CINNAMON CHIPS

4 soft flour tortillas
Butter flavor non-stick cooking spray
1/2 t. cinnamon
1/4 cup sugar
1/4 t. Molly McButter

Preheat oven: 350°

Use kitchen scissors and cut tortillas in half (2 at a time, if you prefer) and then cut each half into 3 wedges. Place wedges on baking sheet sprayed with non-stick cooking spray. In small bowl, mix together cinnamon, sugar and Molly McButter. Generously sprinkle wedges with sugar mixture. Spray wedges very lightly with non-stick cooking spray. Bake in 350 degree oven for 12-13 minutes. These burn easily, so watch carefully.

Entire recipe makes 4 servings.

Grams Of Fat Per Serving
1

Calories Per Serving
119

Fat Free

ORANGE & PINEAPPLE RICE PUDDING

1 cup rice (not instant)
1/2 cup orange juice
1/4 cup sugar
1/2 cup canned evaporated skim milk
1 cup skim milk
1 t. orange peel
1 8 oz. can crushed pineapple
1/4 t. salt

Preheat Oven: 350°

In medium saucepan combine all ingredients and stir over medium heat until sugar is dissolved. Spray a medium sized, deep casserole dish with non-stick cooking spray. Pour mixture into casserole and cover and bake at 350 degrees for 1 hour. After one hour, remove lid and return to oven to cook uncovered for 15 more minutes. Serve warm or cold. It's delicious either way. Great for breakfast.

Entire recipe makes 4 servings.

Grams Of Fat Per Serving   Calories Per Serving
0   165

BLACKBERRY SURPRISE

1\2 cup frozen blackberries
2 T. water
Non-nutritive sweetener to taste
2 t. vanilla, sugar-free instant pudding. Be sure to
buy <u>instant</u>
  and <u>sugar-free</u>.

Place frozen blackberries in small bowl, add water.
Microwave on high for 45 seconds. Time may vary
with microwaves. Thaw the berries thoroughly, do
not cook. Remove from microwave and add
sweetener. Stir and mix sweetener with berries...
mash the berries a little with the spoon while stirring.
Add 2 t. dry pudding mix right from the package.
Mix and stir with berries. Serve and enjoy.

NOTE: Try experimenting with different berries and
fruit. Strawberries are good and also canned
peaches. The amount of water added depends on
the type of fruit you are using. You can also vary
the amount of water and amount of instant pudding
mix to get a thinner or thicker consistency,
depending on how you personally like it. Have fun
with this recipe, it has lots of possibilities.

Entire recipe makes 1 serving.

<u>Grams Of Fat Per Serving</u>   <u>Calories Per Serving</u>
            0   70

CRISPY RICE AND MARSHMALLOW TREATS

4 cups miniature marshmallows
4 cups crispy rice cereal
3/4 cup graham crackers, ground
    (About 12 graham cracker squares) (square = 2 1/2" X 2 1/2")
1 t. vanilla
1 t. Molly McButter

Place marshmallows in large saucepan, sprayed with non-stick cooking spray. Warm marshmallows over low heat to melt. It may be necessary to remove pan entirely from heat from time to time to keep from scorching marshmallows. Stir constantly. When marshmallows are melted, add vanilla and Molly McButter and mix.
In large bowl, combine crispy rice cereal and graham crackers. Pour this mixture into melted marshmallow and stir until all cereal is coated. Turn mixture out into large baking dish sprayed with non-stick cooking spray. Spray a large spoon with non-stick cooking spray and use this spoon to gently press mixture in into baking dish. Allow to cool 20-30 minutes before slicing into servings.

Entire recipe makes 8 servings.

Grams Of Fat Per Serving	Calories Per Serving
less than 1	109

BANANAS WITH CREAM CHEESE CHOCOLATE SAUCE

2 bananas, sliced

<u>Sauce</u>
2 T. fat free chocolate ice cream topping
4 T. lite cream cheese
2 T. sugar

Optional: 2 slices angel food cake

In small bowl combine ingredients for sauce and stir until sugar is dissolved. Pour over sliced bananas.

Optional serving: Slice bananas over a serving of angel food cake and add sauce.

Entire recipe makes 2 servings.

<u>Grams Of Fat Per Serving</u>   <u>Calories Per Serving</u>
            2   204

214

216